Shorter Henry Miller titles
by Capra Press:

ON TURNING EIGHTY (1972)

REFLECTIONS ON THE DEATH OF MISHIMA (1972)

FIRST IMPRESSIONS OF GREECE (1973)

WATERS REGLITTERIZED (1973)

REFLECTIONS ON THE MAURIZIUS CASE (1973)

Henry Miller's
BOOK OF FRIENDS

*A Tribute
to Friends
of Long Ago*

1976
CAPRA PRESS
Santa Barbara

Library of Congress Cataloging in Publication Data

Miller, Henry, 1891 —
Henry Miller's book of friends.

1. Miller, Henry, 1891 —   — Friends and
associates. 2. Miller, Henry, 1891 —
— Biography — Youth. I.   Title.   II.   Title: Book of
Friends.
PS3525.I5454Z518   818'.5'209 [B]   75-38790
ISBN 0-88496-050-1
ISBN 0-88496-051-X pbk.
ISBN 0-88496-052-8 lim. ed.

ACKNOWLEDGMENTS
Cover, "Happy Days," litho by Henry Miller.
Brooklyn photos by Jim Lazarus.
Back cover by Bill Webb.

CAPRA PRESS
631 State Street
Santa Barbara, California 93101

TABLE OF CONTENTS

BOOK OF FRIENDS

Fillmore Place—my favorite street as a child. It doesn't seem to have aged too badly.

CHAPTER ONE

Stasiu

He was the very first friend in my life.

A friend from the street, where we first met, in that glorious Fourteenth Ward I have written about so glowingly. We were both five years of age. I had other little friends in that neighborhood beside Stasiu of course. It has always been easy for me to make friends. But Stasiu was my real friend, so to speak, my pal, my buddy, my constant companion.

Stasiu was what his parents called him. None of us dared call him that because it made him a "Polak" and he didn't want to be thought of as a Polak. His name was Stanley and Stasiu is the affectionate diminutive for Stanley. I can still hear his aunt calling in her sweet staccato voice — "Stasiu, Stasiu, where are you? Come home, it's late." I will hear that voice, that name, until my dying day.

Stanley was an orphan who had been adopted by his aunt and uncle. His aunt, a woman of enormous proportions with breasts

[9]

like cabbages, was one of the sweetest, kindest women I have ever known. She was a real mother to Stanley, probably much better than his own mother would have been had she lived. His uncle, on the other hand, was a drunken brute who owned the barber shop on the ground floor of the house we lived in. I have the most vivid and terrifying memories of him chasing Stanley through the streets with an open razor in his hand, cursing him at the top of his lungs and threatening to cut his head off.

Though Stanley was not his son, he too had an unbridled temper, particularly when one teased him. He seemed to have no sense of humor whatever, even later when he had grown up. Strange, now that I think of it, that "droll" was one of his favorite words. But that was much later, when he had dreams of being a writer and would write me lengthy letters from Fort Oglethorpe, or Chickamauga, when serving in the cavalry.

Certainly as a boy there was nothing droll about him. On the contrary, his expression was usually glum, morose, downright mean at times. If I angered him, as I did occasionally, he would chase after me with clenched fists. Fortunately I could always outrun him. But these chases were long and full of terror, for I had an unholy fear of Stanley when he lost his temper. We were about the same size and build, but he was much the stronger. I knew that if he ever caught me he would beat me to within an inch of my life.

What I did on these occasions was to outdistance him and then hide somewhere for a half-hour or so before sneaking home. He lived at the other end of the block in a shabby three-story building much the same as ours. I had to be very wary sneaking home, for fear he was still on the lookout for me. I didn't worry about meeting him the next day because these rages of his always subsided in due time. When we met it would be with a smile, a wry one from Stanley, and shake hands. The incident would be forgotten, buried — until the next time.

One might wonder how I became such good friends with a kid like this, who on the whole was a rather unsociable lad. It's hard for me to explain myself, and perhaps it's best I don't try. Maybe even at that early age I felt sorry for Stanley, knowing he was an orphan, knowing his uncle treated him like a dog. His foster parents were poor too, much poorer than my parents. There were many things I owned, toys, tricycle, guns and so on, to say nothing of the special privileges that were granted me, which made Stanley jealous and envious. He was particularly annoyed, I remember, because of the beautiful clothes I wore. It didn't matter to him that my father was a boss tailor, rather well-to-do for that time, who could afford to indulge his fancy. Myself, I was rather embarrassed and often ashamed of wearing such sumptuous raiment when all the kids I associated with were virtually in rags. These duds my parents thought looked so fetching on me made me look like a little Lord Fauntleroy, which I hated. I wanted to look like the rest of the gang, not like some freak from the upper classes. And so, now and then, the other kids would jeer at me as I walked hand in hand with my mother, and call me a sissy, which made me wince. My mother, of course, was insensitive to these gibes and to my feelings as well. She probably thought she was doing me a great favor, if she thought about it at all.

Already, at that tender age, I had lost all respect for her. On the other hand, whenever I went to Stanley's home and met his aunt, that delicious hippopotamus, I was in seventh heaven. I didn't realize it then, but what made me so happy and free in her presence was that she was affectionate, a quality I didn't know mothers were supposed to possess in dealing with their off-spring. All I knew was discipline, criticism, slaps, threats — or so it seems as I look back on this stage of my life.

My mother, for example, never offered Stanley a huge slice of rye bread smeared with butter and sugar, as did Stanley's aunt when I visited his home. My mother's greeting to Stanley usually was: "Don't make too much noise and be sure to clean up when you've finished playing." No bread, no cake, no warm slap on the back, no 'how's your aunt' or anything. Just don't

[11]

make a nuisance of yourself was the idea she conveyed by her manner.

Stanley didn't come very often to my home, probably because he sensed the unfriendly atmosphere. When he did it was usually because I was convalescing from some illness. I had all the child's illnesses, by the way, from chicken pox to diphtheria, scarlet fever, whooping cough, the measles and what not. Stanely never had any illness that I knew of. One couldn't afford to be ill in a poor family like his.

And so we often played on the floor below, where my grandfather sat on a bench making coats for my father, the boss tailor of a Fifth Avenue establishment. We got along well, my grandfather and I; I could communicate better with him than with my father. By comparison, my grandfather was a cultured gentleman, who spoke a beautiful, impeccable English which he had learned during his ten years in London as an apprentice. It was a pleasure, when the holidays were on and all the relatives gathered together, to hear my grandfather discourse on the state of the world, on politics — he was a Socialist and a Union man — or to listen to his tales of adventure as a boy when wandering through Germany in search of work. As Stanley and I played parchesi or dominoes, or some simple card game, my grandfather would hum to himself or whistle a tune from some German song. It was from his lips that I first heard *"Ich weiss nicht was soll es bedeuten das Ich so traurig bin . . ."* He had one song called "Shoo-fly, don't bother me," which he sang in English and which always made us laugh.

There was one game we played with toy soldiers and cannons which roused us to fever pitch; we would shout and scream with excitement as we battered the enemy to pieces. The racket we made never seemed to disturb my grandfather. He went right on sewing and pressing his coats, humming to himself, getting up now and then to yawn and stretch. It was a back-breaking business sitting on a bench all day making coats for my father, the boss tailor. Now and then he would interrupt our play to ask us to go to the saloon at the corner and fetch him a pitcher of lager beer. He would always offer us a little, very little, saying it would not harm us.

If I were not in good enough condition to play games I would read to Stanley from one of my fairy tale books. (I knew how to read before going to school.) Stanley would listen for a while and then beat it. He didn't like to be read to. At that age he wasn't much of a reader; he was too healthy for such a pastime, too restless, too full of animal spirits. What Stanley enjoyed, and I too when I was well, were rough games in the street, and we knew many of them. If football had been the rage then, as it is now, he might have become a football player. He liked "contact" games in which you shoved the other fellow about or knocked him flat on his ass. He liked to use his fists too; when he got angry and put up his dukes it was always with his tongue sticking out, like a viper. Because of this habit he often bit his tongue, which would set him to howling and scowling. Most of the kids on the block were afraid of him, except for one little Jewish boy whose big brother had taught him the manly art of self-defense.

But my apparel — I have to use a high-falutin word for it. One day when my mother was taking me to the doctor, me rigged out again in some outlandish costume, Stanley planted himself square in front of my mother and exclaimed: "Why does he have to get all these fancy things? Why don't somebody dress me up like that?" Upon saying which he turned his head away and spat. It was the first time I saw my mother soften up. As we walked on — she was carrying a parasol, I remember — she looked down at me and said hurriedly: "We'll have to get something nice for Stanley to wear. What do you think he'd like?" I was so bewildered by this about-face that I didn't know what to answer. Finally I said: "Why don't you get him a new suit? That's what he needs most." Whether Stanley ever got the suit I don't recall. Probably not.

There was another boy in the neighborhood whose parents were very well-off and who also used to dress him up in grand

[13]

style. They even had him wear a derby on occasion, along with a little cane. What a sight in that poor neighborhood! To be sure, he was the son of a Congressman, and a spoiled brat to boot. All the kids made fun of him and would tease him unmercifully, trip him up if they could, call him filthy names, imitate his mincing gait, and make him miserable in every possible way. I wonder what became of him in later years. With a start like that it seems to me it would be hard for anyone to become anything worthwhile.

In addition to his other qualities Stanley was also a good liar and a thief. He stole barefacedly from the fruit and vegetable stands and, if caught red-handed, would invent a pitiful story about his folks being so poor that he never had enough to eat.

One of the special privileges I enjoyed, one which Stanley never shared with me, was to attend a matinee vaudeville show every Saturday at a local theatre called "The Novelty." I was about seven years old when my mother decided to let me enjoy this privilege. First, of course, I had to do some chores — wash dishes, scrub the floor and wash the windows. I was then given a dime to buy myself a seat in the gallery — "nigger heaven," we called it. I usually went alone, unless my little friends from the country happened to be visiting us.

Though Stanley never got inside a theatre, the two of us used to enjoy an imaginary spectacle at a burlesque house nearby called "The Bum," a name invented because of its evil reputation. Saturday nights we would first inspect the billboards displaying the soubrettes in tights, then take a stand near the box office, hoping to catch some dirty jokes the sailors might make as they stood in line for their tickets. Most of the jokes were over our heads, but we got the drift of them nevertheless. We were inordinately curious to know what went on in there when the lights went up. Did the girls really strip to the waist as they said? Did they throw their garters to the sailors in the audience? Did the sailors take the girls to the nearby saloon after the performance and get them drunk? Did they go to bed with them in the

[14]

rooms above the saloon from which there always came great sounds of merriment?

We would question the older boys in the street about these matters, but seldom got satisfactory answers. They usually told us we were too young to be asking such questions, and then they would laugh in a most significant way. We knew a little bit about the fucking business because there was a girl named Jenny, just a wee bit older then us, who would offer her body to any and all of us for a penny a crack. This performance usually took place in Louis Pirossa's cellar. I don't think any of us really got it in her. Just to make contact sent shivers up and down our spines. Besides, she always remained in a standing position, which is not the best position for beginners. Mere urchins that we were, we referred to her among ourselves as a whore. Which did not mean that we treated her badly. It was simply that we marked her out as different from the other girls in the neighborhood. Secretly we admired her for her boldness. She was a very likeable girl, rather good-looking and easy to talk to.

Stanley didn't figure strongly in this cellar game. He was shy and awkward, and, being a Catholic, felt guilty of committing a grave sin. Even when he grew up he was never a lady's man, never a skirt chaser. There was something austere and severe about him. I am certain that he never went with a girl until he ran into the woman who was to become his wife, and to whom he remained faithful. Even when he joined the cavalry and wrote me long intimate letters about his life in the barracks he never spoke of women. All he acquired in those four years with Uncle Sam was how to roll the dice and guzzle it. I'll never forget the night I met him in Coney Island upon his release from the service. But that's for later . . .

Summer nights in New York, or Brooklyn, as it happened to be, can be wonderful when you're a kid and can roam the streets at will. On a very hot night, after we had worn ourselves out playing "cops and robbers," say, we would finally settle down on Stanley's doorstep, eating cold sauerkraut and cold frankfurters

[15]

which he would swipe from the icebox. We could sit there talking
for hours, it seemed. Though Stanley was rather the silent type,
with a long, thin face rather dour in expression—something on
the order of Bill Hart, the cowboy idol of the silent screen—he
could also talk when in the mood. At seven or eight the man who
was later to write "romances," as he called them, was always
recognizable. To be sure, he didn't talk love, but the ambiance
in which he set his little tales was poetic, imaginative and romantic. He was no longer the street urchin looking for trouble,
but a dreamer longing to escape from his narrow environment.
He loved to talk of far-off places like China, Africa, Spain, Ar-
gentina. The sea had a special appeal for him; he wanted to be
a sailor when he came of age and visit these strange, distant
lands. (In another ten years he would be writing me about
Joseph Conrad, his favorite author, who was also a Pole but who
had chosen to write in English.)

During these talks on the doorstep he was indeed another
Stanley. He was softer and gentler. Sometimes he would interrupt himself to tell me of his uncle's cruelty, show me the welts
on his back, where his uncle had beaten him with the razor strop.
I remember him telling me how furious he made his uncle by
refusing to cry; he would simply clench his teeth and scowl, but
never let out so much as a whimper. It was typical of Stanley.
That's how he went through life, taking his punishment but
never showing what he felt. It was a tough life from the very
start and it ended as miserably as it had begun. Even his "romances" were doomed to failure. But I am getting ahead of
myself . . .

Born in America, Stanley nevertheless had many of the char-
acteristics of an immigrant. For example, he never spoke Polish
in front of us though we knew he did at home. If his aunt spoke
Polish to him before us he would answer in English. He was
ashamed to speak Polish in our presence. There was something
slightly different about his use of English compared to ours; he
did not use the gutter language we indulged in with the same ease

[16]

or fluency as the other boys. He was also more polite than we were and showed respect to adults, whereas we other kids seemed to enjoy being vulgar, disrespectful and careless about our speech. In other words Stanley had good manners even though he was just a gutter snipe like the rest of us. Stanley hadn't cultivated these habits, they were a result of being brought up by people from the Old World. This touch of refinement in Stanley was something of a joke to us, his friends, but we never dared mock him because of it. Stanley not only could hold his own with the best of us but, as I said before, when irritated or offended he was a holy terror.

There was another thing about Stanley I should touch on — his jealousy. While still living in that same neighborhood I became acquainted with two youngsters my own age who lived in the country, as we called it, though actually it was a suburb of Brooklyn. Every now and then my parents invited these boys to stay with us; later on I would visit them — "in the country." Joey and Tony were their names. Joey soon became one of my great friends. Stanley, for one reason or another, didn't show much warmth toward my new-found friends. He made fun of them at first because their ways were different from ours. He pretended that they were stupid and too innocent — country bumpkins, in other words. The truth was that he was jealous, particularly of Joey whom he sensed I had a great affection for. It was as if Stanley and I were blood brothers and no one had the right to come between us. It was true, of course, that there was no other boy in the neighborhood about whom I felt as I did about Stanley. His only rivals were older boys, whom I regarded as my idols. I was a hero worshiper, a born hero worshiper, no doubt about it. And I still am, thank God. Not Stanley, however. Whether it was because he was too stiff-necked, too proud to bow his head, or just plain jealous, I can't say. He had an eye for the flaws and failings in others and was rather good at lampooning and ridiculing those he disliked. All his efforts were in vain where my idols were concerned. To me, no matter what anyone said,

[17]

my idols were made of pure gold. I saw only their virtues; if they had any defects I was blind to them. It may sound rather ridiculous, but I believe I see things in very much the same way today. I still look upon Alexander the Great and Napoleon as extraordinary human figures, men to be admired no matter what their faults. I still think reverently of Gautama the Buddha, Milarepa, Ramakrishna, Swami Vivekananda. I still adore such writers as Dostoievsky, Knut Hamsun, Rimbaud, Blaise Cendrars.

There was one older boy whom I regarded not as a "hero" like the others but more as a saint — not a Saint Augustine nor a Saint Bernard, but a Saint Francis. That was Johnny Paul, an Italian born in Sicily. To this very day I think of Johnny Paul with the utmost tenderness, sometimes, to be frank, with tears in my eyes. He must have been eight years older than Stanley and I, which is a great deal in the calendar of youth. As best as I remember he delivered coal for a living. He was of dark complexion with very bushy eyebrows set above two dark, glowing eyes which burned like hot coals. His clothes were always dirty and ragged and his face covered with soot, but he was clean inside, clean as a hound's tooth. What got me about him was his tenderness, his soft, melodious voice. The way he would say, "Hello Henry, how are you today," would melt me. It was the voice of a compassionate father who loved all God's children. Even Stanley had to succumb to his charms, which were nothing more than a fundamental good nature and a humility that was utterly sincere. Stanley even liked the fact that he was a "wop," whereas Louis Pirossa and some of the other "wops" were beneath Stanley's attention.

At the age of seven or eight an older boy can play a great role in one's life. He is a father without being a father; he is a companion without being a pal or a buddy; he is an instructor without the forbidding lineaments of a teacher; he is a father-confessor without being a priest. He can mold a boy's character or set him on the path, so to say, without being meddlesome,

[18]

pompous or sententious. All these things Johnny Paul was to us. We adored him, we hung on every word he said, we obeyed him and we trusted him. Would that we could say the same of our own fathers, our own teachers, our own priests and counselors!

Sitting on the doorstep in the cool of the evening Stanley and I often wracked our brains to explain to ourselves why Johnny Paul was so different from the other young men of his age. We knew that he had had no schooling, that he couldn't read or write, that his parents were of very humble origin, nobodies so to say, but not trash. Where did he get his good manners, his kindness, his gentility, his forbearance? For, above all things, Johnny Paul was a tolerant individual. He had the same regard for the worst among us as for the best; he played no favorites. What a great, great thing that is, especially if one has been reared among narrowminded, prejudiced, bigoted individuals, as most of our elders were, including the hypocritical minister of the gospel, old man Ramsay, who lived next door to Stanley and sometimes chased him down the street with a horsewhip.

No, we were not taught to admire, much less venerate, such simple souls as Johnny Paul. How interesting that a mere boy should discover what constitute the sterling qualities in an individual when his parents and teachers recognize only the counterfeit. I cannot resist dwelling on this theme because I have believed all my life that children have more to teach adults than the other way round. The person who has never dealt with children is a spiritual cripple. It is children who not only open our hearts but our minds as well. It is only through them, only in seeing the world through their eyes, that we know what beauty and innocence are. How quickly we destroy their vision of the world! How quickly we transform them into the image of us short-sighted, miserable, faithless adults! To me the root of all evil is our parents, our elders. And I don't mean simply bad parents, ignorant parents: I mean parents as such, all parents. Johnny Paul opened my eyes; not Jesus, not Socrates, not the Buddha. Needless to say, I didn't realize the gift he had made us

[19]

until many years later, when it was too late to thank him.

Since Stanley's parents couldn't afford to give him the spending money he required to purchase his little luxuries, Stanley found himself a job running errands for Mrs. O'Melio, the little old lady who loved cats. She was regarded as soft in the head or eccentric by the neighbors because she kept from thirty-five to forty cats on the flat tin roof over the veterinary's stable. From my window on the third floor I could look down on her feeding this motley assortment of felines twice a day. I didn't share the opinion of my parents who called her a nut; I considered her a good soul. I was the more convinced of this when she asked Stanley if he would run her errands, for which she would give him a dollar a week. I knew she did it because she wanted to help Stanley. I wished that someone would offer me a job like that; I longed to do something useful. I didn't need the extra money, because my parents saw to it that I had everything I needed. I was embarrassed and ashamed that I should have everything I wanted while my companions lacked all but the bare necessities. One by one I gave my toys away to those who craved them. When I finally gave away the beautiful drum my parents had given me for my birthday I was severely punished. More than that, I was deeply humiliated. My mother had taken it into her head to recover some of the beautiful toys I had given away. So what did she do? She took me by the ear and dragged me to my friends' homes and made me ask for my toys back. She said that would teach me not to give away my presents. When I was old enough to buy my own things I could then give away whatever I chose. Presents cost money, I was to remember that. I did indeed remember her words, but not in the way she intended.

I made a few feeble efforts to find work but with no success. Why did I want work, my prospective employers would ask. Your parents are well-off, aren't they? Whereupon I would hang my head and slink off. In truth I didn't want work, I only wanted to imitate Stanley. To be honest, I hated work. All I wanted was to play. If I had had the means I believe I could have been a

[20]

playboy all my life. I never had that desire to make an honest living, which everyone is supposed to have. I was born with a silver spoon in my mouth and I wanted to keep it there. I didn't think then that I was a spoiled brat, nor did I think, as I did later, that the world owed me a living. When I realized that it didn't, it was a rude awakening.

Playing in the street had a more sinister aspect at times than one might think with regard to children's pastimes. One of our chief delights was to go on marauding expeditions, dealing death and destruction, so to speak. Stanley was the leader fortunately, because only he, it seemed, knew when to call a halt to our depredations. Stanley could influence and control the wildest ones among us, and I must say it was no mean job since some of the gang had truly murderous instincts.

One of these was a snot-nosed lad named Alfie Melta whose old man was a cop. There was something of the fiend about this youngster. He had no brains at all, and no language. He was a low-grade moron with a touch of evil in his make-up. He wasn't crazy, like Willie Payne, nor a half-wit like Louis Pirossa. He was an out-and-out dope who opened his mouth only to emit bloody oaths and filthy objurgations. He could lie like a trooper, throw fake epileptic fits when necessary, have tantrums at will, and was an absolute dare and a sneak, a rat, a coward to boot. When he wished to express something, anything, the muscles of his face would twitch and his eyeballs would roll like dice in a box. He could turn anything into a weapon, even a toothpick. He had the ingenuity and the inventiveness of a good second-story man. He loved the sight of blood; even if it was his own blood it made him gleeful.

His counterpart, and a wonderful asset on our raids, was Sylvester, the son of a hod-carrier who seemed to be on a perpetual spree. His name fitted him superbly—it had an angelic sound. It was a name you caressed in pronouncing it. He had the look of innocence itself, the look of a cherub by Fra Angelico, a cherub just sprung from the arms of Jesus, or the Virgin Mary.

[21]

Such beautiful violet eyes! Such lovely golden locks! Such a fair complexion with just a tinge of pink in his cheeks! The women in the neighborhood adored him, would pat him on the head, offer him candy and sweets of all kinds. He talked like a little angel too, devil that he was. When he accepted a compliment or a gift he would lower his big, violet eyes with their long, curly lashes, and blush. Little did these adoring mothers know what a monster they were dealing with.

Sylvester had "cool," as we say today. He was never ruffled, never disturbed, never rueful, never touched by regret or remorse. It was Sylvester who was entrusted with the dangerous jobs; it was Sylvester who robbed the church; it was Sylvester who gave false alarms; Sylvester who upset baby carriages for kicks; Sylvester who stole from the blind; Sylvester who set fires to stores. There wasn't anything Sylvester would not do, if he had a mind to. The difference between him and Alfie Melta was that Sylvester played it like an artist. His deviltries were all *actes gratuits*. Clever as he was, however, he was to end up in the penitentiary before coming of age.

Sylvester's doings were born of pure, ice-cold malice. Alfie Melta, on the other hand, was hot-blooded, impetuous and reckless. He hadn't brains enough to figure things in advance. He wanted action, spectacular action, no matter what the risk. He ended up in a reformatory before he reached his teens.

How it was that Stanley could influence and control these little monsters I never could figure out. Perhaps it was because they feared him, perhaps because they admired him. For Stanley too had some of their baser qualities. Some of that brutality his uncle had shown toward him had to be worked off on others. Some of that daily humiliation he suffered at home had to be inflicted on others. No, Stanley was far from being an angel. He was a good kid who was always getting the dirty end of the stick. He needed to rub some of that shit under other people's noses. His young, tender heart was already becoming rancorous.

Stanley was at his best when leading us to invade enemy

[22]

territory. In every poor neighborhood there are feuds between one side and another. In our case it was perpetual war between the North side and the South side. We were of the North side, which was like being on the wrong side of the railroad tracks. Our pleasure was to invade the swanky South side, beat up a few helpless sissies and return with a few captives whom we tortured to the best of our ability. I don't mean by torture that we pulled their nails out or cut them to ribbons; we were content to steal the clothes off their back, or rip them to shreds, swipe their pocketknives and watches, if they had any, douse them under the fire hydrant, give them a bloody nose or a black eye, and so on. Alfie Melta always had to be restrained because he liked to see blood. A great coup would be to rob a South side boy of his bike. The greatest enjoyment we got from these escapades was to send the other side home in tatters and bawling like two-year-olds.

Most of the boys in our gang were Catholics and were sent to a Catholic church on the North side. My parents, though they practiced no religion, insisted on sending me to a Presbyterian church, run by a wealthy English minister, on the South side. I often had to run the gauntlet going to and from church. Because I was bright, well-dressed and came of a good family the church brethren regarded me as a little angel. For reciting the 23rd Psalm by heart I was given a little gilt-edged Bible, or New Testament rather, with my name embossed in gold letters on the cover. I never dared show this testimonial to any of the gang except Stanley. Stanley was puzzled over the award of such a gift. In his church, he said, no one but the priest was allowed to read the Bible. Neither did Catholics go to Sunday school, only to mass, and that at an ungodly hour. What was Sunday school like, he wondered. I tried to explain it to him but he only shook his head. "Your's ain't no church," he said, "it's more like a kindergarten."

One day I told him I had seen a moving picture in the basement of the church. "What's that?" he asked. I explained just what I had seen on the screen. "A Chink walking across the

[23]

Brooklyn bridge." "And anything else?" said Stanley. I confessed there was nothing much else. Stanley was silent a moment, then said: "I don't believe it." To tell the truth, I hardly believed it myself, though I had seen it with my own eyes. The superintendent, another Englishman who always wore a cutaway with striped trousers, had explained to us that a man named Thomas Edison had invented this miraculous moving picture machine, and that we were very fortunate to have had the privilege of seeing one of the first films ever released. He spoke of the "silent screen," a phrase which impressed me greatly for some unknown reason. At any rate, for Stanley that was one of the differences between his church and mine—that you could see moving pictures for nothing in the basement.

Perhaps we would never have discussed religion, Stanley and I, had it not been for this Chink walking across the Brooklyn Bridge. Now, among other profound subjects we would discuss on his doorstep of an evening, was this business of religion. Did we go to confession, he wanted to know. What did I know about the Virgin Mary? Did I believe in devils and angels? Who wrote the Bible and why wasn't he allowed to read it? Was I afraid of going to Hell some day? Did I take Communion? I confessed I didn't know what Communion was. He was taken aback by this. I asked him to explain it, but all he could say was that it was like eating Christ alive and drinking his blood. The thought of drinking blood made me queasy. But Stanley quickly assured me that it was only imitation blood—just some kind of red wine which the priest blessed first. I got the impression that Catholics were an outlandish sort of breed, something like refined savages.

He told me he had an uncle living in New Jersey somewhere who was a priest. "He can't marry," said Stanley. "Why?" I asked. "Because he's a priest. It's a sin for a priest to marry." "Our minister is married," I said, "and has children." "He's no priest, that's why," said Stanley. I couldn't understand why it was such a sin for priests to marry. Stanley volunteered an explanation. "You see, a priest can't go near a woman," he began.

[24]

He meant "sleep with her." "A priest belongs to God; he's married to the church. Women are temptation to a priest." "Even good women?" I asked naively. "All women," said Stanley emphatically. "Women lead us into temptation." I didn't quite understand what this word temptation implied. "You see," said Stanley, "if a priest went to bed with a woman she would have a child, and the child would be a bastard." I knew the word bastard, I had often used it in calling a fellow names. But this bastard was a new kind of bastard to me. I didn't press him further on this because I didn't want to appear to be totally ignorant. I began to realize that Stanley knew a lot more about religion than I did, even if I could recite the 23rd Psalm by heart.

Stanley was not only more sophisticated than yours truly but he was a born skeptic. It was he who opened my eyes, and nearly broke my little heart, by informing me that there ain't no Santa Claus. It took quite a bit of explanation to convince me of this. I was the sort who believed in anything: the more impossible it was, the quicker I believed it. I was an apt pupil for St. Thomas Aquinas. However, in the Protestant churches they didn't talk much about saints. (Was it because the saints were such sinful guys at bottom?) As I remarked earlier, Stanley hadn't much use for fairy tales; he preferred reality. I doted on fairy tales, especially the grim, terrorizing ones, which gave me nightmares. Later in life I see myself marching to the public library on Fifth Avenue, reading day after day the fairy tales from every country in the world.

There was another myth which Stanley almost knocked out of my head a year or so later, and that was that storks deliver babies. I had never thought much about this subject, since babies aren't particularly interesting to little boys. When I asked Stanley where they did come from he said, "from the mother's belly." This sounded absolutely incredible to me. "How do they get out then?" I jeered. That Stanley couldn't answer. It didn't occur to him that babies came out of that little crack between the legs which we saw on Jenny Payne. Nor was he sure how they were

[25]

made. All he could say was that it had to do with parents sleeping together. It's not so surprising, when you think of it, that his little brain couldn't make the connection between babies and sleeping together. Many primitive peoples didn't make the connection either. In any case, for once I was the one who was skeptical. I thought of asking my mother, but then I knew in advance she would never answer a question like that. She could never answer anything which profoundly interested me. I soon learned not to ask questions at home . . . I had a hunch Johnny Paul might know the answer, or even Jenny Payne, but I was too shy to put such a question to them.

Jenny Payne . . . Jenny had a brother who was off his noodle. Everybody called him "Crazy Willie." He was a big, gawky, gangling idiot about fifteen years of age whose speech was limited to a dozen words or so but who wore a perpetual Steeplechase smile. He was quite a problem to his family, naturally, since they couldn't always keep an eye on him. When he wandered into the street he was mercilessly tormented; it was considered good sport to take advantage of a helpless lubber like Crazy Willie. Stanley always defended the poor bugger. Why, no one could understand. Stanley could calm him down when he threatened to run amok; he was even able to hold communication with him. Sometimes he would bring Willie a slice of rye bread with butter and jam on it, which Willie would gobble down in two mouthfuls. Willie often imagined that he was a horse, and he would act like a horse, to our great amusement. He would put his head down and snort and whinny, exactly like a real horse, or he would gallop and frisk his imaginary tail. Occasionally he would let out a tremendous fart, upon which he would do a pirouette, then stand on his hind legs and paw the air with his front ones. His parents were kind folk who didn't have the heart to put him away. In those days the insane asylums weren't filled to overflowing as they are now. Many who should have been there were walking the streets or kept prisoners at home. In our own respectable family we had several crazy

[26]

specimens, including my mother's mother.

One of the serious problems Willie's parents had to face was how to prevent Willie from masturbating in public. It seemed that Willie usually had the urge to give an exhibition around six o'clock in the afternoon. Willie would usually take his stand outside his window on a narrow ledge one story above the street level. Suddenly he would open his trousers and pull out his prick, which was of no mean size, and with an ecstatic grin and a few unintelligible exclamations, would jerk away for dear life. At this hour the trolley car which ran through our street would be jammed with workers returning home. If it were summertime the trolley would be an open one with a running board on either side. Seeing Willie performing his antics the motorman would stop the car and the passengers would shout and wave to Willie in hilarious fashion. Soon a crowd would gather and the police would be summoned. Willie wasn't afraid of the police, but his parents were. After an incident of that sort Jenny Payne would blush and lower her head as she passed us by. As for Willie himself, the worst that would happen to him would be a good strapping from his old man. Until the next time . . .

Soon now I will be moving to another neighborhood. Stanley will drop out of my life for a while — but he will return, and in a different guise.

The ninth year of my life is approaching and with it the end of my first Paradise on earth. No, the second Paradise. My first was in my mother's womb, where I fought to remain forever, but the forceps finally prevailed. It was a marvelous period in the womb and I shall never forget it. I had *almost* everything one could ask for — *except friends*. And a life without friends is no life, however snug and secure it may be. When I say friends I mean *friends*. Not anybody and everybody can be your friend. It must be someone as close to you as your skin, someone who imparts color, drama, meaning to your life. Something the other side of love, yet including love.

That's why I write this, to tell about those friendships which

[27]

meant so much to me. I realize that I have touched on some of these relationships before, in other books of mine. I relate them again now in a different way—not as the solipsist I am often accused of being but *as a friend*. The difference between the Paradise of the womb and this other Paradise of friendship is that in the womb you are blind. A friend furnishes you with a thousand eyes, like the goddess Indra. Through your friends you live untold lives. You see in other dimensions. You live upside down and inside out. You are never alone, never will be alone, even if every last one of your friends should disappear from the face of the earth.

The German physicist Fechner said that we live three lives: one in the womb, one in the world, and another in the beyond. He overlooked the multiple lives we live in and through others, because of others. Even in prison we do not live a solitary existence. Was it Socrates who said: "Who so would live alone must be either a god or a wild beast"?

Once I wrote that I was born in the street and raised in the street. I was speaking then of the glorious 14th Ward which I am soon to leave for "the street of early sorrows." Today I prefer to think that we who lived in the street, we for whom the street was everything, created these streets, created these homes, created the very atmosphere we breathed. We did not come into a world ready-made: we invented our world. I cannot leave it without paying homage to it once again.

Until I went to France I never realized why I was so attached to this little world of my childhood. In Paris I discovered a replica of that microcosm called the 14th Ward. In the poor quarters of Paris where I wandered penniless and unknown for many a day and month I saw all about me the sights of my childhood days when I was a spoiled brat. Again I saw cripples, drunks, beggars, idiots roaming the streets. Again I made friends of poor and humble origin, real friends who saved my life time after time. Again I felt that I was in a man-sized world, a human microcosm suited to my taste. There in Paris, in its shabby, squalid streets teeming with life, I relived the sparkling scenes of my childhood.

It is so hard to believe that poverty too can have its glamorous side. I don't recall anyone in that old neighborhood whom I thought of as well-off except the family doctor and the minister of our Presbyterian church. The shopkeepers probably made a decent living, but they were certainly not rich. No one owned an automobile because there were no such animals in existence then, or if they did exist they belonged to some other planet.

When I think of those streets now they are usually in full sunshine. Everywhere bright awnings, parasols, flies and perspiration. No one is running or pushing and shoving. The streets are becalmed, swimming in heat, and slightly perfumed with rotting fruit. At the veterinary's a stallion is pinned to the earth and his balls are being cut off. I can smell the scorched, seared flesh. The shanties, which are already caving in, seem to be melting. From them issue dwarves and giants, or little monsters on roller skates who will grow up to become politicians or criminals, whichever way the dice roll. The brewery wagon with its huge kegs of beer looks gigantic. There are no skyscrapers, no high rise buildings. The candy shop just a few doors from our home is out of Charles Dickens, and so are the spinsters who run it. Mrs. O'Melio is moving amidst her thirty-eight cats of all stripes and denominations with a big bowl of food in her hand. There are two toilets in our house; one is in the garden and is just a plain old-fashioned shithouse. The other is upstairs on our floor and has running water and a wick floating in a little cup of sweet oil to light when it is dark. My bedroom is just a cell with one window giving on the hallway. There are iron bars protecting it, and through the iron bars come most of my nightmares in the form of a huge bear or a fearsome monster out of Grimm's fairy tales. After dinner in the evening my father would dry the dishes which my mother washed at the sink. One evening he must have said something to offend her for suddenly she gave him a ringing slap in the face with her wet hands. Then I remember distinctly hearing him say to her: "If you ever do that again I'll leave you."

[29]

I was impressed by the quiet, firm way in which he said it. His son, I must confess, never had the courage to talk that way to a woman.

I mentioned my proclivity for reading. One of my favorite books, one I read over and over again, was *Stories from the Bible*. They were Old Testament stories largely, with unforgettable characters such as King David, Daniel, Jonathan, Esther, Ruth, Rachel and so on. I wondered sometimes why I never met any people like that in the street. I sensed that there were two worlds, the world of heroes and heroines which I found in books and the world of ordinary people like my parents and all the other parents in the neighborhood. There were no flaming prophets, no kings, no young heroes with slingshots amongst us. There was that crazy preacher with the horsewhip, old man Ramsay, but he was no Ezekiel. I tried to tell Stanley about these wonderful people who inhabited the Bible but he dismissed them as being fictions of the Protestant religion. "The priest never speaks about such people," he said, and that was the end of that.

Just as there are frontiers which separate nations so there were boundaries which marked off our world from neighboring ones. Those who lived beyond these boundary lines were potential enemies. We were always wary, always on guard, when we stepped into their precincts. In our own little world everything was understandable, including cruelty, thievery and epilepsy. We were one big family composed of micks, wops, kikes, heinies, Polaks and an occasional Chink. The important thing was to keep alive. The next important thing was not to get caught. The world is an abstract term for something which exists only in the mind. The earth is real, and the sky and the birds of the air. For us there were no "airs," as in Greek philosophy. There was only ozone which, taken in deep draughts, was good for the lungs.

As I say, Stanley had moved to New Jersey or Staten Island. His aunt had divorced her husband, the barber, and married an undertaker. I wouldn't have known it had not Stanley waved to me from the driver's seat of the hearse which happened to pass through our street one day. I could hardly believe my eyes.

We too had moved to a new neighborhood which at first had little appeal for me. The boys of this new neighborhood lacked the charm and the character of the boys of the old neighborhood. They seemed to be replicas of their parents who were dull, strict and extremely bourgeois. However, I soon made friends — I have a gift for that, it seems. In school I became friends with one boy who was to remain a life-long friend and to play quite a part in my life. He was a born artist. I saw him only at school, unfortunately.

Now and then I had a letter from Stanley and now and then we met, to undertake one of those shady operations Stanley now let himself in for. We would take the ferry to Staten Island and during the course of the journey Stanley would discreetly drop over the side of the boat a little box. In the box was an abortion. Perhaps he received some extra spending money for doing his new uncle this favor — he never said. A little later he was to do even shadier things. Somehow he managed to get himself a job as an interpreter at Ellis Island. Instead of helping his compatriots, Stanley robbed them. He had no sense of shame about it either, which really surprised me. His attitude was — if I don't do it someone else will.

During these few years in which we were growing up we saw very little of one another. Stanley never spoke of girls, I noticed, whereas I was deeply involved and would continue to be so for many years to come.

Finally the day came when Stanley joined the Army — the cavalry, to be more precise. And from now on I began receiving letters from Ft. Oglethorpe, Ga. or Chickamauga.

All the Army ever taught Stanley was how to drink and how to gamble. The day he got his release from the Army we met — in Coney Island. He must have had his full pay with him for he spent money like a trooper. He drank beer, nothing but beer, steadily from the time we met. Naturally he tried everything — from the rides to the shooting galleries. We were loaded down with prizes he won—he was a sharpshooter in the Army. About three in the morning, we checked in at a shabby hotel somewhere in Brooklyn Heights. He went to bed drunk as a pope and cleared his head next morning by drinking stale beer.

He was a different Stanley alright. Tough now and ready for trouble at a moment's notice. Despite his condition, he still had a mind for literature. His two favorites, of whom I was to hear a lot later, were Joseph Conrad and Anatole France. He wanted to write like them, either one, it didn't matter.

Some more time elapses, during which he learns to become a printer. And the next thing is marriage—to a rather dull-looking Polish girl about whom he had never breathed a word.

By this time I too had married. As chance would have it, we found ourselves living only a few blocks apart, he on the wrong side of the tracks, as they say.

Now of course we saw one another more frequently. Nights, after dinner, Stanley often dropped around to chew the fat with me. Both of us were trying to write, and each was critical of the other. We were terribly serious about it all too. I was still working as employment manager for the telegraph company.

To prove to myself that I was indeed a writer I wrote a book about twelve messengers during a three week vacation. I don't think I even mentioned it to Stanley; why I don't know. Possibly I didn't want to embarrass him. Of course I never dreamed of showing it to him for he would have picked it to death.

What I remember vividly about this period are Stanley's two boys. They were scarcely a year apart in age. Always well-dressed, polite, immaculate and painfully well-behaved. They were always deathly pale, as if made of alabaster. Stanley often brought them along of a late afternoon. What they did during these visits was a mystery to me. They remained out of sight until called for, as children should. They never quarreled, soiled their clothes or complained about anything.

When I think of their behavior now I wonder that they did not arouse my wife's admiration. They behaved exactly according to

[32]

her principles. But for whatever reason, she paid them little attention. Nor did she ever inquire after Stanley's wife, who, though a good person, was definitely not very interesting.

It was when I got to know June that Stanley pricked up his ears. Though he didn't approve of my doings he sympathized with me. And, he was extremely discreet. Little by little he watched the whole drama unroll.

One day, out of the blue, he said to me: "Do you want to get rid of her?" Meaning my wife. I probably nodded yes. "O.K. Leave it to me," he added. And that was that. Not another word.

I don't believe I gave it serious thought. It was just a whim of his, I supposed. But it wasn't.

What role he played with my wife I don't know. I can only imagine that he said something similar to her. At any rate, one fine morning, when June and I are sleeping together — in my own home, to be sure — suddenly the rolling doors are pulled open and there stands my wife, her girl friend from upstairs, and the girl's father. Caught in *flagrant delictus,* as they say. A few days later my wife's lawyer serves me with court papers — for divorce.

Now how had I been caught like that? Stanley was very clever. He had suggested to my wife that she and the child take a vacation — and then return unexpectedly. To make sure that my wife *was* taking a vacation I had accompanied her to the little town she was stopping at. I had returned on the next train and, happy as a lark, had called June to give her the good news. That's how we happened to be caught in bed.

What I remember about this scene of the three witnesses is that, despite her embarrassment and her desire to leave the house as soon as possible, I managed to persuade June to stay. I fixed us an excellent breakfast — just as if nothing had happened. June thought this rather strange on my part. Said something about lacking feeling.

I never understood how Stanley could be sure I would bring June to the house that night. "My instincts told me so," he replied when I questioned him about it. To him it was a simple, cut and dried affair. All he demanded of me was that I would have no regrets later. I never did.

Of course I had to quit living with my wife. I have related elsewhere the many places June and I lived at and the people we were beholden to.

It must have been soon after the divorce that June began to press me to give up the job with the telegraph company and start writing. The idea was that she would provide the necessities in one way or another. And so, one day, I did just that. I quit the telegraph company and swore that henceforth I would be a writer and nothing else.

I won't attempt to recount my struggles here. Suffice it to say, they were Gargantuan and never-ending. Finally came the day when, alone and penniless, we faced the grim reality that we had failed. What was worse, we were hungry. We were kicked out of the place we lived in.

To this day I don't know what impelled me to do so but I thought of Stanley as my last resort. I had never borrowed a cent from him nor he from me. I knew I couldn't ask him for money — but perhaps he could put us up for a week or so until one of us found something to do. With that in mind I dragged June along to see Stanley. They had never met and, strangely enough, Stanley had never expressed the least desire to meet this woman with whom I had become so infatuated. I was a little uneasy about their meeting — they were at opposite poles.

Fortunately June seemed to appeal to Stanley's chivalrous side. He was overgenerous. He decided to give us the mattress of his bed so that we could lie on the floor in the parlor. His wife and he would sleep on the springs.

It was understood, to be sure, that June and I would diligently look for work and leave as soon as possible. Though it was a bit awkward, a bit uncomfortable, things went all right for the first few days.

Usually June and I left in the morning together — to look for work. Shameless though it sounds, I must confess neither of us ever did look for work. She sought out her friends and I mine. We were lazy and inconsiderate, and what is worse — ungrateful. It's this I feel bad about, even today, some fifty years later.

Fortunately, things didn't last long at this rate.

In some unknown way Stanley discovered that we were doing nothing. One evening, when we both arrived together, Stanley simply said: "The game's up. Pack your things and I'll take you to the subway." That was all. No display of temper, no histrionics. He had found us out and he was through with us.

Shamefacedly we packed our things, said good-bye to his wife and kids, and followed him down the stairs. (It seemed to me that I detected a grin on his wife's face during these proceedings.)

At the subway station Stanley handed me a dime, shook hands and said good-bye. We scuttled down the steps, took the first train that came along and then looked at one another blankly. Where would we go now? At what station would we get off? I let June decide.

That was the last of Stanley. I never saw or heard from him since. The last episode has left a nasty scar in my memory. I was guilty of doing something one ought never do, especially to a friend. And Stanley was my first friend. No, I have never forgiven myself for my shameless behavior, for my betrayal of a friend.

What became of Stanley I don't really know. I heard in a roundabout way that he had gone blind, that he had put his sons through college — and that's all.

His life must have been a very drear, lonely one. I'm sure he hadn't much interest in his wife. I know he hated his job of printer. And I am sure he never had the least luck with his writings. What I might have done for Stanley is a question, since I was never able to help myself. But I had Fortune on my side. Time and again, when all seemed hopeless, I was rescued, most often by a perfect stranger. Stanley had no one working for him, least of all the gods.

[35]

Épreuve d'artiste   Broken Dreams   Henry Miller   1973

A fountain used to be here where the bicycle riders assembled on Sunday mornings to ride to Coney Island and back.

CHAPTER TWO

Joey and Tony

Just to say their names makes me think of the Golden Age. Unfortunate the man who has never known a Golden Age. I am still in that period between seven and twelve. Living now in a new neighborhood, on Decatur Street in the Bushwick section. "The Street of Sorrows" I dubbed it later. But at this time I am not too unhappy. To go to Glendale, a suburb of Brooklyn, with my mother and sister, was an event — a joyous one. We could walk to their home in an hour's time. For us it meant walking into the country. For me it was my first contact with nature — and with art.

John Imhof, the father of Joey and Tony, was an artist. He made watercolors (usually at night when every one had gone to bed) and he also made stained glass windows for the little churches in the vicinity. How my parents became acquainted with the Imhofs I don't know. Probably through the "Saengerbund" (Singing Society) where they made so many friends.

When I think of these two little friends now they scarcely seem real to me. They were more like something out of a child's book. They had qualities none of us city boys possessed. For one thing, they were always bright and gay, always full of enthusiasm, always discovering things. They talked a different language than we others. They talked birds, flowers, frogs, snakes, pigeon eggs. They knew where to look for bird's nests. They raised chickens, ducks, pigeons, and they were at home with them.

They always had something new, something interesting, to show me on my arrival. Perhaps they had acquired a peacock, or else another puppy, or an old billy goat. Always something live and warm.

The moment I arrived I had to accompany them — either to show me some new nest eggs or some new stained glass window their father had just made. I was at that time totally uninterested in stained glass windows and watercolors. I never dreamed that one day I too would be sitting up until all hours of the night making watercolors. Anyway, John Imhof was the first artist to appear in my life. I can recall hearing my father pronounce the word artist. He was very proud of his friend John Imhof. And every time I heard the word a commotion took place inside me. I hadn't the slightest conception of what it meant. I only know that the word art did something to me. By contrast, Tony and Joey were already familiar with the names of the great religious painters and they had big, heavy books in which the works of these painters were shown. Thus from an early age I knew such names as Giotto, Cimabue, Fra Angelico and such like. Sometimes, to tease Stanley, I would reel these names off.

The Imhofs were Catholics. And so I became familiar with the names of the saints as well as the great painters. I often accompanied Tony and Joey to church. I must confess I didn't like the atmosphere of the Catholic Church. Nor was I able to believe any of the doctrine which they tried to impart. I particularly disliked the portraits they kept at home of the Virgin Mary, of John The Baptist, and of Jesus who died for us hanging on the cross. All this was terribly morbid to me. However, I soon noticed that my little friends didn't take these things to heart. They weren't born Catholics, so to speak, such as you would find in Spain, Sicily or Ireland. They could just as well have been Turks.

This Glendale was just a tiny village, bordered on one side by a golf links and on the other by two Catholic cemeteries. Between these lay a valley which we never penetrated. It was more like a No Man's Land. The streets were wide and flanked by huge shade trees. Every house was fenced in. At the corner of their street lived the Rogers family, consisting of an ailing Aunt and a young man in his late teens who was to my friends what Lester Reardon and Eddie Carney were to me. This Rogers lad was on his way to becoming a golf champion. My little friends were only too honored to caddy for him. Myself, even to this day I have never had the least interest in golf. I don't understand the game any more than I do football.

There were so many things I didn't understand, it seems to me. By comparison, Tony and Joey were extremely sophisticated. They took a delight in opening my eyes.

I have always envied those born in the country. They learn the essentials of life so much more quickly. If life is hard for them it is also healthier. From the city boy's point they may seem re-tarded but they are not. Their interests are different, that's all.

Until I met Joey and Tony I had never held a bird in my two hands, never knew what it was to feel the warmth and the trem-bling of a tiny live creature. With my friends I soon learned to handle mice and snakes. Nor was I afraid when a goose would go after me.

Just doing nothing was such a wonderful treat. To lie in the sweet smelling grass on warm earth and watch the clouds drift or the birds wheel overhead. The days were mapped out for us, to be sure, but there was always plenty of time between chores to laze around.

Even as a youngster the Christian religion never meant a thing to me. It reeked of the grave. It spoke of evil, sin, punishment. It was morbid and death-like. I never derived peace or joy from it. On the contrary, it often filled me with terror, especially the Catholic faith. The confessional was a huge joke to me. A hoax, a fraud. No, everything about the church seemed made for nitwits.

There were bizarre characters in this community. One man, named Fuchs, I believe, was what my friends called a "hundski" picker. That meant he went about all day with a shortened broomstick on the end of which was fastened a spike with which he gathered dog turds. He carried these turds in a sack on his back and when he had a sufficient supply he brought them to a perfume factory where he was well paid for his efforts. He spoke a strange language, this Mr. Fuchs. Of course he was a bit light in the head. He knew it too. That's what made his antics more droll. He was, to be sure, a devout Catholic and was forever blessing himself or muttering a "Hail Mary." He tried to get us to work for him but we couldn't see it. As for work, there were plenty of odd jobs my friends could take. They were never at a loss for pin money. Usually they gave half their earnings to their mother.

It wasn't long before I detected something amiss between the father and mother. Mrs. Imhof, it was obvious to all, had begun to hit the bottle. Her breath was always boozy, her steps uncertain. She would do silly things too, which one could not help but notice. The conversation between her and her husband was indeed limited. Usually he was complaining that things were going to hell. And they were. Fortunately there were two other members of the family who did their best to help—Minnie, the elder daughter and Gertrude, who was about my age.

Why the sudden rift between these two who had been married a good twenty years was uncertain. The boys maintained their father was in love with an old sweetheart in Germany who had begun writing him letters. They said he had even threatened to leave them and go to Germany to live with his sweetheart.

(Which is exactly what he did do a few years hence.)

Usually the father retired fairly early. He did not go to sleep immediately. He made watercolors by the light of a student lamp. We had to pass through his room (on tip toe) to go to our bedroom. It always gave me a holy feeling to see Mr. Imhof bent over a pad of paper with a brush or two in his hand. He seemed not to be aware of our presence.

Evenings after dinner we usually played chess. Joey and Tony were quite good at the game; they had been taught by their father. More than the game I liked the chess pieces themselves. They were elaborate and expensive — from China, I believe. I have played the game at intervals all my life but never succeeded in becoming a good player. For one thing I lacked the necessary patience. For another I was too reckless. It didn't matter to me whether I won or lost. I enjoyed the beauty of the moves — aesthetics rather than strategy.

Sometimes my friends permitted me to read to them from my books. I hadn't lost the habit. Generally they fell asleep before I had gone very far. Next morning they would ask me innocently to tell them what I was trying to read to them the night before.

Near the city limits of Glendale, near the German-American section of Brooklyn called Ridgewood, was a place called Laubscher's. It was a huge beer hall, with pool tables and bowling alleys, and plenty of parking space for horses and buggies. There was always an arresting aroma of stale beer, horse piss, horse manure and other pungent odors. This is where the elders congregated once a week — to sing, to dance, to guzzle it. We were always taken along and once there left to our own resources. I must say they were jolly evenings, unlike anything we know of today. They loved to sing — in chorus. And to dance. At that time the waltz was the favorite dance. But they danced all the other dances too — the polka, the schottische. And the square dances. These were something to behold.

While all this activity was going on we were raising hell on our own. Many was the half-empty glass of beer we polished off. It

[41]

was an excellent place to play cops and robbers, for instance. And with all the running and sweating, it did us no harm to consume as much beer as we did. Sometimes we would set up the pins in the bowling alley—for free—because we felt good. That usually earned us some change and some good turkey sandwiches. All in all these were marvelous weekends, with the entire family walking home (or reeling) and singing at the top of our lungs.

I often wondered as we passed the Rogers' house (which was by no means a mansion) if we were not in danger of waking old Mrs. Rogers. About the singing—the songs they sang on these occasions—I mean the coming-away songs—were familiar to everyone.

I suppose the one most frequently sung was *"Wien, Wien, mur du allein. . . ."* Even today, if I am in the right mood, that is mildly intoxicated, grossly sentimental, thoroughly mellow and in love with the world, tears fill my eyes. I become what my friend Alf always nicknamed me—*"un pleurnicheur."*

There are certain American folk tunes which have the same effect on me—notably Stephen Foster's songs. No one, it seems to me, can sing "Way Down Upon the Swanee River" or "My Old Kentucky Home" with dry eyes. I should add another, one composed by Theodore Dreiser's brother—"On the Banks of the Wabash Far Away." Paul Dressler was the name his brother adopted, and a most lovable character he was.

For some reason the mention of these songs reminds me of the music class in the high school I attended. The teacher, Barney O'Donnell, was a jovial Irishman in his sixties, who made no attempt to teach us music. He simply sat down at the piano, ran through a few keys in his own inimitable way, looked up and said —"What'll it be this morning?" This meant we could choose whatever we liked to sing. And sing we did—with heart and lungs. It was the best day of the week for us. We were always grateful we had Barney O'Donnell with us. Between songs he taught us a few Irish (Gaelic) phrases, such as "Faugh a balla!"

[42]

(Clear the way) or "Erin go bragh!" (Ireland Forever). If only the other subjects could have been taught us in this light-hearted fashion! Perhaps then we would have retained some of that deadly knowledge they were trying to teach us and which most of us seemed unable to swallow.

In those days nearly every home seemed to sport a guitar. Even my mother, who had little music or poetry in her veins, had learned to play the guitar. At an early age I was taught to play the zither. On these weekends I can still recall the strange old woman, gypsy-like, who sat in a corner of the big beer parlor, strumming the guitar or zither. And always a glass of beer beside her. The songs she sang were anything but gay. But she seemed to be appreciated. Her voice was dark and throaty and the expression on her face as she sang was one of utmost sadness. People would stop and listen, shake their heads, and offer her another drink. Years later, in Vienna, I saw her double. She was seated in a little café, scantily clad, shivering with the cold. And looking fit for the grave. But when she played the zither it was unforgettable. All this to say that at the Imhofs they had both a guitar and a zither, which no one played.

Joey and Tony were almost of the same age, Tony being the younger. Tony, even at that early age, had something of the priest about him. (Later in life he was to become one.) He was forever telling us not to do this, not to do that, or that he would tell the Father (meaning the priest) of our immoral conduct. We all three slept in one big bed. Joey and I had acquired the habit of buggering one another. We thought nothing of it, but to "Turk," as we had nicknamed Tony, we were committing a grievous sin. Sometimes we tried to bugger him, but it was useless —he was incorruptible.

There was another thing I was guilty of at bedtime. Next to our bed slept their elder sister Minnie, who was several years older than any of us. When we thought she had fallen asleep I would sneak out of bed, pull the covers off her, and raise her nightgown so that we could have a good look at her quim. She al-

[43]

ways threatened to tell my mother the next day but never did. This too, of course, was an unholy deed in Tony's eyes. No matter how much we twitted and teased him about his Puritanical attitude we could never shake him. If there is such a thing as a born priest then Tony was one.

Finally Mr. Imhof did up and leave for Germany, to the dismay and complete puzzlement of my mother. "He was such a good man, such a fine man," she kept repeating. "How could he do such a thing? How could he leave his children like that?" Obviously it never occurred to her that there was a powerful force in life called love and that in the name of it people did strange and unpredictable things.

At any rate, it wasn't long after their father had flown the coop that the family moved to Bensonhurst where they occupied a much larger house with ample grounds about it. How this happened, how they were able to make such a change, I never found out. Perhaps Mr. Imhof hadn't been such a bad one as people imagined. Perhaps he had left some money behind so that they would not be in want.

The new place was a delight. Now they could really fend for themselves. They had chickens, geese, ducks, pigs and more pigeons of course. Also dogs and cats. In the yard was a big skup. There was room for a tennis court as well, but no one knew anything about tennis. They had of course plenty of vegetables and beautiful flower beds. In a way Mr. Imhof's going was a windfall. The two daughters were bitter about their father's behavior and absolutely unforgiving. But not Tony and Joey. They took his departure as a matter of course. Joey even said he would have done the same thing had he been in his father's shoes.

Minnie, the elder daughter, was as I said before, a few years older than us. She was a rather homely girl, and none too bright. It wasn't long before she fell for the wiles of a young Polish fellow who soon made her pregnant. This, to be sure, was another calamity. I remember the day the boys told me about it. They made no recriminations against her Polish boy friend. He

[44]

was a decent sort, they said, but not serious. He had refused to marry Minnie. He said she had no proof that it was his kid she was carrying under her belt. Anyone who knew Minnie knew this was untrue, that Minnie couldn't possibly carry on with more than one man at a time.

So eventually the child was born—out of wedlock—and accepted as a member of the family. She too was not too bright, but she was bold, shameless, reckless, and led her mother around by the nose while still a little tot. She was hardly in her teens when the same thing befell her as did her mother. The difference was that she didn't care.

The younger daughter, Gertrude, was totally different from any of the family. She was very good-looking, healthy, alive to the fingertips and extremely respectable. As soon as she was able she went to work and became the main support of the family. As I grew older I became more and more attracted to her. I mistook her curiosity for intelligence, her liveliness for full-bloodedness. I had only to go out with her once or twice — to the theatre or a dance—to realize that she was not at all the creature I had believed her to be. As a matter of fact, I quarreled violently with her and eventually grew to despise her. If her brother Tony had the makings of a priest, she had the makings of a nun, or rather a Mother Superior. Beneath the glamour she was cold as ice, unforgiving, uncharitable, and downright stupid. What became of her I don't remember, but I assume she married and had children.

But in those early days when we visited the Imhofs in Bensonhurst all went relatively smoothly. The boys had part-time jobs, the family lacked for nothing, and we did pretty much as we wanted to. A short distance away, by trolley, was an unforgettable place called Ulmer Park, where there was an outdoor theatre; the audience sat at little tables in the sunshine and ate and drank during the performances. My mother had begun taking me to this wonderful spot when I was still quite young. It made a tremendous and lasting impression on me. For here,

[45]

in this out of the way corner of the world, came the famous stars of Europe — clowns, trick cyclists, slack wire men, trapeze artists, opera singers, magicians, acrobats, comedians, tightrope walkers and so on. Later in life I wondered how it was that my mother had the sense to take me to such a place. Here I heard Irene Franklin sing "Redhead."

And not far from this place was another equally unforgettable place — Sheepshead Bay. Here in a cove many boats of all kinds were anchored. But the principal attraction of the place were the wonderful fish restaurants. Here one could always get oysters on the half shell, raw clams, clam chowder, soft shell crabs, and every variety of fresh water and sea fish imaginable.

Not so many years later, when I was miserably in love and seemed abandoned by all my friends, I would take to my bike first thing in the morning and ride and ride until I was exhausted. I called my bike my only friend. If it were possible I suppose I would have slept with it. But the point is that there was only a few years between the happy, carefree days with Joey and Tony and these present miserable, almost unbearable ones. All because of a girl. All because she didn't return my love. And so, setting forth on the bike I would often find myself in Bensonhurst, Ulmer Park or Coney Island. Only now all was different. I was alone, forlorn, of no use to the world or myself.

In Bensonhurst I could no longer find the place where the Imhofs once lived. Where had they gone? Meanwhile Mr. Imhof had died — in Germany. I am sure his sons took it with their usual equanimity. It was my mother who made a fuss over his death, weeping crocodile tears and muttering to herself what a good man he was, that it never should have happened to him, and so on. After a time, I learned in a roundabout way that both boys had become letter carriers. After a few years Tony quit to become a priest in some distant parish but Joey remained to become superintendent of the post office he worked in. He also married a school teacher, much to my surprise.

The last time I saw him was some ten or fifteen years later. It was during those desperate days with June. In despair I visited him to borrow what I could. He was the same old Joey, the same good friend. He gave me ten dollars and said I could forget about paying it back. I had expected to receive more but was thankful for this much. Hadn't one of my good friends handed me a nickel when I asked him for subway fare? I was getting to the point where pennies counted. Soon I would become an out and out panhandler. I had lost all pride. It was solely a matter of survival.

Epreuve d'Artiste   Early Music   Henry Miller 1973

View of 181 Devoe Street
where my first love lived.
The white house, third from
the left, is the one.

CHAPTER THREE

Cousin Henry

He was like the King of 85th Street

(Manhattan) and I was like the Prince of the 14th Ward
(Brooklyn). Every summer our parents arranged that we stay
two or three weeks at one home or the other.

My cousin Henry was anything but a king by nature, yet he
commanded respect and the obedience of the boys in his neighborhood. It was through him that I first realized I must be different from the other boys, perhaps even a genius, though I
showed no aptitude for creativeness as a writer, painter, actor.
But I *was* different. Something about me, even at that early
age, elicited the admiration and the loyalty of other boys my age.

When Cousin Henry announced to his cronies that Henry
Miller would be arriving next week it took on the importance
of a State visit. I was an emissary from another world. I had
something different to offer. Besides, we were blood cousins, and
that carried weight.

[49]

I can see myself arriving of a summer's day and being gradually introduced to all the members of the gang, each one a
unique character, in my estimation. I wondered what was so different about myself as to win their instant favor. One thing I
noticed almost immediately was the way they hung on my words.
It was as if I spoke another language which they could only dimly
understand but which enchanted them. Aware of this, I was fearful lest they take me for a little gentleman. Nothing was more unthinkable in this neighborhood than a "gentleman." There were
simply no such animals about. (Suddenly I thought of one of my
boyhood idols, Lester Reardon, who had the air of a young
lion—an *aristocratic* young lion. I wondered how he would fare
with these young hoodlums.)

My cousin Henry, as I started to say, had nothing of the king
about him. Already, at that early age, a melancholy aura hung
about him. He was very quiet, withdrawn and introspective.
In my presence he seemed to come alive—he even looked happy
at times.

It was through Cousin Henry that I first became aware of the
other sex. I had hardly arrived when he introduced me to a
charming young creature whom they all called "Weesie" (after
Louise, I suppose). She was presented to me as if to say—"Here,
here's something nice for you. Have a good time together." It
was all done so naturally, so matter of factly, that I failed to be
embarrassed. I immediately assumed the role I was supposed to
play. There were other girls besides Weesie, of course, but
Weesie was like the Queen of the harem.

In those days summertime was different than today. For one
thing, I believe it was actually hotter then than now. One sought
the shade, whether a cool room or the cellar of a building. One
made ice-cold drinks of all kinds. And, willy nilly, one became
more sensual, more passionate, more eager to explore. And the
girls were not averse to such explorations. I had difficulty at first
suppressing my reactions. Everything here happened too easily,
too naturally. Of course, I didn't know what moral and immoral

meant — I never heard those words at home or on the street — but I could recognize the difference between one kind of behavior and another.

However, when in Rome do as the Romans. Which I did, to everyone's delight. The situation was rendered more strange — *and* more delightful — by reason of the fact that where I came from the two sexes occupied separate worlds. No one thought of girls as something different. Except for those little intermissions in the cellar — as with Jenny Payne — no one seemed the least concerned about sex. We might enjoy watching the monkeys hump one another in the zoo, but there it ended. Sex was more of a healthy, pleasurable sport. As for love, it was something utterly unknown to us.

Summertime. A glorious time, despite the flies, the mosquitoes, the cockroaches. The street seemed wide open, like a corpse just dissected. It was a perfect Ufa setting, what with the relatives and friends hanging out of their windows, usually only half dressed. Take my father's sister, for example — Aunt Carrie. A good-natured slut who was a little too fond of her beer. She was a most easy-going creature, loose with her tongue, and content to gossip from morning till night. My mother looked upon her with open disgust. Indeed, my mother looked upon the whole neighborhood as a bed of sin — and what was worse, as unclean. Idlers were something new to her. And women who drank. No, she did know one or two who drank, but their drinking was done in secret. You might well imagine my mother saying to herself — "If one has to go to the dogs one should do it in as refined a way as possible."

But 85th Street was neither refined nor secretive. Everything was out in the open. That's why it appealed to me. Add to this that there was an air of sophistication which was unknown in the 14th Ward.

I should have explained that my father had three married sisters living in this street — he himself came from one of those houses.

[51]

It was only in this vacation time that he ever saw his sisters. My mother wouldn't dream of inviting them to our house. Later on I got to thinking of his sisters as belonging to Tchekov's gallery of characters. They were kind, gentle, sympathetic, but poorly equipped educationally. Their husbands were not much better. One of them, Uncle Dave, to whom I later became greatly attached, could not even sign his own name. Yet he was a born American. He was a baker by trade. His wife, Aunt Amelia, another sister, was most lovable. Unfortunately, she was to die of cancer at an early age. They all seemed to be afflicted with incurable diseases, yet they maintained a joyous air, were fond of coarse jokes and loved the little things of life. Beer cost practically nothing in those days and was consumed in great quantities—without anyone seeming to be too drunk. They drank because they were thirsty and because the beer tasted good. They never drank just to get drunk, nor to drown their sorrows.

My Uncle Henry was my cousin Henry's father. A big, hulk of a man, with a thick Germanic accent, he sat around most of the time in his fireman's wool undershirt. With the "growler" in front of him, to be sure. My mother found him too absolutely disgusting. It's true he had no manners, but then what use was there for manners in such a place? He had been my father's boon companion when they were young men. That's how he happened to marry one of my father's sisters, I guess. To see these two men side by side now one wondered how there had ever been anything between them. Strangely enough, it was the theatre which had enchanted them both. They had seen the greatest actors and actresses from abroad in their time. They even enjoyed Shakespeare when played by renowned artists. It was in the evenings, seated about the table, that I caught snatches of their adventurous lives. To me it opened up a New York which was glamorous and romantic. A filthy street like 14th Street now became an avenue of importance, full of color and of great names. One felt the affinity which then existed between Europe and

America. Immigrants were still pouring in in great numbers and many of them becoming rich or famous. All the names which we look back upon nostalgically were then living idols. One could encounter them in the flesh in any bar or saloon or in the lobby of a hotel such as the Waldorf.

Because of his size, his hairiness, his usually unshaved condition, Uncle Henry looked comically fierce. He was, of course, tender as a lamb, and the way he spoke to his son was a revelation to me. The impression I got was that Cousin Henry was something very precious and one could not do enough for him. In some ways Cousin Henry resembled me. At any rate, we understood one another thoroughly. Nothing he said or proposed ever surprised me. He was a strange boy for his age. I mean, he behaved like a man and always seemed to act reasonably. He seldom laughed or told jokes. To him I was something of a phenomenon. He could not get over the fact that I was a great reader. I always brought my favorite books along and, at the first favorable opportunity, I would read aloud for them. The results were usually disastrous. One by one my listeners fell asleep. Some snored heavily. But I did not seem to mind. I continued reading, probably for myself now.

In those days I could reread a book a dozen times if it interested me. I was familiar with stories from the Bible, Aesop's Fables, Aladdin's Lamp, Homer's Iliad and Odyssey, and such like literature. It was very familiar stuff to me, required no effort to read. Why others didn't instantly like it always mystified me. Robin Hood and Helen of Troy were like intimate friends. I found I had to do a lot of explaining when reading these things to my little friends. They always wanted to know why or why not. Very vexing questions.

The girls who listened, on the other hand, seemed to be enchanted. I rose a few inches in their estimation because of this predilection of mine. The other boys, apparently, fed on the cheap magazines for boys, such as Nick Carter, Buffalo Bill and so on. Myself, I was never able to read one of these magazines.

[53]

They had nothing to offer me.

Among all his peculiar friends there was one fat fellow whom I will call Louie and who, for some strange reason, reminds me now of one of Herman Hesse's unforgettable characters. Louie, however unprepossessing in appearance, somehow exerted a charm which no one was immune to. His talk was suave and smooth, rather above people's heads, his manner absolutely bland, his curiosity about even the most trifling things, absolutely enormous. He seemed to know about everything and to be happy in dispensing his knowledge. With it all he was extremely modest and humble. One regarded him as a walking encyclopedia. Like babes, we fed at his breast. He was also somewhat psychic, this Louie. For example, after stunning us with his account of life on the lost Atlantis, he might suddenly turn to one of the boys, pointing a finger at him, and warn him to take good care of himself because he felt there was a good likelihood of the boy getting pneumonia a few days hence. Or he would predict a great fire somewhere, which later events would prove true.

Despite these abilities Louie was very much a child still. To offer him a piece of candy or a piece of cake made him very happy. All that was needed to round out the picture was to put a balloon in his hand. But that may also have changed his character, for Louie was many-sided. With a balloon in one hand and a stick of candy in the other Louie might have easily been transformed into a child murderer. It should also be remembered that Louie was one thing with us and quite another with grown-ups. Like so many angelic types, there was something sinister about Louie, about his ability to please and to deceive his elders. The worst I ever heard about him, to be sure, was his obsession for strangling cats.

One night Cousin Henry asked me if the noise kept me awake. "What noise?" I said.

"There's a crazy man in the next street who comes home drunk every night and beats his wife up. You can hear her for blocks around."

"I've never heard anything," I said.

"Good." Pause. "O Henry," he began, "I wanted to tell you something. Weesie told me to tell you that she leaves the door of her room unlocked. She's hoping you'll pay her a visit some night."

"I didn't think it was as serious as all that," I said, not knowing what to do or say.

Cousin Henry now proceeded to tell me how to reach her room, which was a rather elaborate affair. I said I would visit her immediately.

Just as he had said, her door was ajar. A faint light came from the interior. I opened the door and walked in on tip toes. Weesie greeted me from a dark corner where her bed was. She spoke in a natural tone of voice, as if to assure me that there was nothing to fear.

I advanced slowly and timidly to her bedside. She put on a soft light and sat up in bed.

"You wanted me to come?" I said.

"Of course," she replied. "I've been waiting to see you for days. I want to talk to you — about many things."

These last words reassured me. If it was only talk she wanted I could provide plenty of that.

"Henry," she began, "you're so different from the others. I fell in love with you before I ever met you. Your cousin Henry has told me a great deal about you. He worships you, you know."

I didn't know, but I nodded affirmatively.

Weesie continued. "I'm a little older than you, that's what makes it easy for me to talk to you freely. I feel you could teach me things. Some of the books you mention, I would love to read them. No one around here reads such stuff."

I was embarrassed, yet not too much so. I had never been placed in such an exalted position before. The strange thing was it was a girl I was talking to. A few years later, after I had been studying the piano, I would astound her with my ability. Now it was words — only words I had at my disposal. I must have told her

[55]

a lot of rubbish, but it pleased her. She said if I felt like it, I could get in bed with her and talk all night. I didn't know how to interpret this. I thought it better to remain outside the bed. She didn't seem to care which way it went. That made me still more comfortable—and loquacious. I was waxing strong when all of a sudden there came a loud noise from an adjoining room. It was her mother. We decided I had better go. I gave her a quick kiss and found my way back to my room.

I didn't wonder much about the event, strangely enough. Living with Cousin Henry nothing ever totally surprised me. I know, of course, that from now on there was a secret bond between Weesie and me. I thought vaguely that maybe I would marry her one day.

The following day was a blistering one. We awoke in an atmosphere as if all the ovens were turned on. One by one we instinctively assembled in Cousin Henry's cellar, the coolest spot in the house. We came equipped with marbles and tops and dice. We also had greasy packs of playing cards. Anything to pass the time. It was the girl's task to make cool, delectable drinks. And to keep out of sight as much as possible.

This morning Weesie greeted me with an extra warm smile and a hug. I was aware for the first time that the dress she wore clung to her figure. It was made of a very soft material, very feminine, which women seldom wear. To my genuine surprise, she said, as she pulled away from me—"I don't want you to answer me immediately. Tomorrow or the next day will do. What I would like to know is what you think about God. Do you believe there is one? Do you like him? Don't tell me what they told you in church—I know all that crap—Tell me what you yourself honestly think. Do that for me, won't you?"

The hot sultry air, the way her dress clung to her body, the taste of her lips, all combined to give her words another connotation. It was a most unusual question, in any event, and especially from a girl her age. It was the first time the subject had come up since those days when Stanley and I talked on his doorstep in the evenings.

What I started to say was that in posing this million dollar question Weesie seemed to be really saying — "It's so damned hot today, why don't we take our clothes off and make love? I've been wanting you to fuck me ever since you arrived. But you always seem to have more important things on your mind."

How can I explain this seeming indifference on my part? Was it simply that I was too young or was it an aspect of that quality of being "different"? Or was it just a natural purity? I am baffled to explain it, as I look back on it. It wasn't that Weesie was unattractive or lacking in seduction. She wore very few clothes, no panties, and was forever exposing herself. Maybe she should have been another two or three years older than she was. There was no question but that the difference in age counted. Had she been twenty or twenty-one the whole picture might be different. But she wasn't. Besides, had she been that much older she wouldn't have been playing with us in the cellar.

I make no mention of the other girls. Each of the gang seemed to have a girl of his own. To me they were dull and decidedly uninteresting.

At that time the neighborhood was definitely Germanic, with a scattered Bohemian contingency living on the margin. There were plenty of saloons, restaurants, pool parlors and dance halls. I doubt there were any brothels. It was an eminently respectable neighborhood, coarse, and vulgar in many ways, but respectable nevertheless.

One difference between Henry's life and mine was that he attended no church. His parents had no use for religion and Cousin Henry was left to decide for himself. When he came to visit me I took him with me to Sunday School. He was extremely interested, surprised how free and easy it was. What also pleased him was the burlesque house, which of course neither of us attended. But we did go to the Vaudeville Theatre Saturday matinees. The theatre was something unknown to him and he was at home in it immediately. What he also liked was to roam the streets with me.

[57]

They were quite different from those in his own neighborhood and they had a strange fascination for him.

I forgot to mention a little incident at the Presbyterian Church I took him to. The minister of this church was English and well off. Rather aristocratic and definitely condescending. As we were leaving that afternoon he suddenly came up to us and asked who our friend was. I told him. "And what denomination does he belong to?" he asked genially. "To none," I promptly replied. "He's an atheist."

"An atheist, is he," repeated the minister. "Well, we'll have to do something about that," and laughing to himself he strode off.

Cousin Henry was furious. First, he thanked me for being honest with the minister. But then he let loose his venom because of the off-hand way in which the minister had received the news of his being an atheist. To Cousin Henry being an atheist was almost the same as being an anarchist. You didn't take anarchists lightly, nor atheists either. This was a side of my cousin I had never seen before and it raised him in my esteem. As for myself, there was nothing I cared deeply about.

What pleased Cousin Henry most was Mrs. O'Melio and her cats. Like Stanley, he had a great respect for a woman who would give so much of her time and attention to these creatures.

He was equally fascinated by the veterinarian below Mrs. O'Melio. He could stand for hours watching the doctor castrate a stallion. These were things which simply did not exist in his neighborhood. He said it was a pity Louie wasn't along. Louie would appreciate such things.

It seems as if there were more shops, more fruit stands, more bakeries in my neighborhood. And I was on speaking terms with all of them, including Mr. Daly who ran the fish market of his own. Now and then he would throw me a few heads of fish he was cleaning, saying — "Here, give them to that Mrs. O'Melio woman for her cats."

Gradually it dawned on me that there was one thing I didn't have to worry about — work. Already, they were talking of fixing up Cousin Henry in the pipe-case factory where his father worked. One would never suspect that this big, gross man, his father, could turn out such beautiful and delicate pipe cases. Of course it was a period when pipes were in vogue, not cigarettes. The meerschamm pipe especially, which improved in color from smoking. (I remember receiving one, and prizing it, for my 21st birthday.)

I had another Uncle Henry who also worked in a factory, was also a big, heavy man, and did delicate work. This Uncle made tooth-picks which were carried on one's watch chain. They were either of gold or pearl-handled, and rather expensive.

Both businesses reflected the manners of the day — the solid bourgeois, cheap in his tastes, flashy, ultra-respectable.

There were things about my cousin Henry I found difficult to understand. His attachment for, or affection, if you like, for Alfie Melta. Alfie, as I have said before, was a born liar, a sneak, a sadist and a coward. Henry seemed fascinated by his ability to become a gang leader. He was right. A little later Alfie would become a gangster, a rather notorious one, and remain in the limelight until cut down, stabbed to death by another gang leader, who in turn would be shot to death in some dark alley. It's curious, this gang business. As simple as North and South. A kid has no choice. He's either for or against. He either does or he doesn't. *He's got to belong,* that's the imperative thing. Nor does he do the choosing. He has to choose the side he's born on, whether good or bad. Why there must be a North and a South is a matter of climate and different ways of life. Inevitable, you might say. And so, from early on, a guy is taught to love and hate, to kill what he doesn't like.

If Alfie was nothing to brag about neither were many of the others. My idols were exceptions, rare birds indeed in a corrupt world. And what saddened me a bit, though I never showed it, was that Cousin Henry never seemed to notice these idols of mine, never questioned me about them. How could he overlook Johnny Paul?

[59]

In both neighborhoods we had the same sort of material —
dumbbells, morons, idiots, lunatics, incipient gangsters, and
here and there a potential leader. It wasn't so much the differences between us as the similarities which attracted.

There's where the girls proved better than us. They looked for
individuals, not sheep of the same stripe. But it was almost im-
posssible for a boy to achieve the freedom of a country, say, like
Sweden or Switzerland, or even achieve the neutral attitude of a
Luxembourg or a Lichtenstein. We were committed from birth.
Political pawns, you might say, from which we developed into
political monstrosities, accepting war, accepting corruption and
buggery of every sort.

Every time I returned to visit Cousin Henry I was more con-
scious of the warmth with which I was received. There was no difference in the way his parents treated me from the way they
treated him. All warmth and tenderness. Far different from the
atmosphere in my home.

And then there were those wonderful slices of rye bread with
rich sweet butter and sugar which his mother handed us when we
came home from play. She did it as if we were two little angels.
Never did she suspect, sweet innocent creature, what her two
"good little boys" were capable of. Never would she have believed that we two had killed a boy in a gang rock fight. No, we
looked just the same as ever that day, or perhaps a little paler,
for we were consicous of the crime we had committed. For days
we trembled if there was an unexpected knock at the door. The
police were constantly on our minds. Fortunately none of the
gang knew we were responsible for the killing. We were intelligent enough to keep our mouths shut. Besides, it was an accident
and not a deliberate killing. As soon as it happened we had
sneaked away. We didn't feel very heroic about it either.

But when I think of my Aunt Anna, her good homely face, all
pock-marked from the small-pox, I realize that she was indeed
what one calls a "pure" human being. I am sure that if we had
told her what had happened she would have forgiven us im-

[60]

mediately and shielded and protected us.

Now with my own mother it was quite different. I could never fool her, though I tried many times. I think from an early age she recognized that her son had a touch of evil in him, that he was capable of doing unthinkable things, things which she preferred not to bring to the forefront of her mind. She was a "respectable" woman. Everybody conceded that. Respectability! How I hated that word! Not that it was mentioned much. But it was there, in the atmosphere, poisoning all my thoughts and deeds.

As I look back I wonder — did those respectable elders of ours really believe that we swallowed all that shit they crammed down our throats? Did they really think we were so stupid, so naive, so unobservant? Even in short pants I could read their minds. I didn't have to grow up to become a psychologist to realize that they were handing us nothing but bullshit and that they, being stronger and in power, bullied us into accepting their lies. Some were such obvious liars, such obvious hypocrites! One had to blush for them. And then the pious ones — who only punished you for your own good! What shit that was!

Yes, each time I returned the reception was warmer. Weesie was developing into a real woman. She was filling out. Her breasts were just right. And she had hair under her arms as well as between her legs.

Occasionally we would go to the Carl Schurz Park nearby, sit on a bench or on the grass, and discuss some of those fundamental questions she loved to put to me. I could answer them better in her room, with one hand between her legs. She was lascivious, Weesie, and loved to be fondled. And she always wore such tempting garments, especially that tulle dress I mentioned earlier which clung to her body like a drape.

Weesie wasn't preparing for any higher education any more than my cousin Henry. It would not be long before she became a sales girl at the Five-and-Ten. She had a good mind, Weesie. It was a joy to discuss things with her. How she put up with the louts who formed Cousin Henry's circle of friends I don't know.

[61]

Like so many of the denizens of this neighborhood she was blessed or cursed with an easy-going disposition. Things didn't matter too much one way or the other. Had it not been that I was very shortly to meet my first love I think I might have fallen deeply in love with Weesie. But with the advent of Cora Seward it was impossible for me to look at another girl.

I doubt that I visited my Cousin Henry any longer after entering high school. As I said, his parents were not concerned about higher education. What they needed was an extra breadwinner. And by the time he graduated from elementary school, Henry was just that. There was no trouble finding him a job in his father's factory. Business was good momentarily. And so, like his father, Henry got himself a lunch box and a thermos bottle. They traveled to work together and came home together. I never heard Henry complain that the job was dull or boring or the hours too long.

To me the situation was almost incomprehensible. It was as if he had chosen to go to prison voluntarily. But they were all doing it, in my neighborhood as well as chez Cousin Henry. It was like joining the Army. When the time comes you sign up. No questions.

I must have seen Henry now only at rare intervals — it's all very dim in my memory. I heard about him through a mutual cousin who lived in the same house.

After a few years he married, had two children and moved to the suburbs on Long Island. It was a miserable, God-forsaken place, depressing, morbid, ugly. Here misfortune began to assail him. I did not know how bad it was until I visited him one day. My visit was an act of desperation. We were broke again, June and I. And I had exhausted all the friends I could think of. Then one morning Henry's image came to mind. He had a job, he must have a little dough to spare, thought I. But I was wrong. He was out of work, the factory had closed down. Add to that, that only a few months before, his wife had died. He himself seemed to be in very poor condition.

I sat and listened to his tale of woe. Tears poured down my cheeks as I listened. He was so abjectly helpless. There was no one he could appeal to for help. His friends seemed to have evaporated. There were no more pipe-case factories in operation. People had given up pipe cases along with beautiful pipes.

I had come to borrow a few cents. A quarter would have helped. But he was penniless and I felt guilty for thinking of begging from him. I should have gone home and borrowed money for him, hook or crook. But I too was up against a stone wall.

We left his house together, to walk to the train station. It was a dark, dreary lane, an utterly miserable place. We shook hands, pretended to smile, and said good-bye. And that was the last I saw of Cousin Henry.

Epreuve d'artiste   The Head   Henry Miller   1973

Eastern District High School where I met Cora Seward and graduated in 1909.

CHAPTER FOUR

Jimmy Pasta

In grammar school he was my only rival.

He was athletic-minded like myself, a serious student, and filled with ambition. (He aimed to be President of the United States one day—nothing less). The fact that his father was a cobbler and an immigrant, from Sicily, I believe, only strengthened his ambition. Besides, his old man loved him and would have made any sacrifice for him.

We got along all right, Jimmy and I, but we were not what one would call great friends. The one great friend I had during that school period was Jack Lawton. But he died very early—at twelve or thirteen—of rheumatism of the heart.

The reason our relationship was on the cool side was twofold. Jimmy was a wop and a Catholic and I was a product of that one hundred percent American white collar Protestant tribe which seems to dominate America. Jimmy's friends were all of

[65]

the lower or lowest class. They were all good fighters—some were already getting to be well-known in amateur boxing circles. But perhaps the thing I could least stand in Jimmy was his pride and ambition. He wanted to lead in everything. What's worse, he *believed* these myths and legends about our heroes. One could never convince him that George Washington was a real pain in the ass or that Thomas Jefferson had several children by his Negro slaves.

The teachers, of course, adored him and helped him in every way. No one ever dared make fun of him. His skin was very dark, he squinted out of one eye—and he had an Italian accent.

Jimmy made it a point to be friends with everybody. That was his "political" side. I had not known anyone before Jimmy who was filled with ambition. To me his antics were like those of a freak.

He was always organizing, or raising funds for this or that. At twelve or thirteen he behaved like an adult. It was unnatural. I refused his invitation to join the club he had formed. I never told him about *our* club. He wouldn't have understood the spirit animating us. We weren't going anywhere or getting anywhere, in Jimmy's mind. Everything he did had to have a purpose, be meaningful. Needless to say, that was not the dominating spirit of the Deep Thinkers or the Xerxes Society.

Jimmy also managed to get his name frequently in the local papers. He was always being praised, admired or envied.

Once he ran the marathon. A heart-breaking experience, and rather foolish to undertake—but Jimmy had to prove that he had what it takes.

He was hardly out of school—I think he was going to night school—when there would be pieces in the paper about him giving lectures to Boy Scout groups and others. Headlines reading—*James Pasta lectures tonight on "Loyality and Obedience"* or *James Pasta lectures on "What makes great men."* Stuff like that. My old man used to read these squibs in the papers and tell me in a meaningful way how much he admired Jimmy. "He's going to go far," my father would say. "Not like you," was implicitly understood. He couldn't see any future for me at all.

About the time Jimmy is building a reputation for himself I am training to become a lieutenant or a captain in a boy's brigade called "Battery A" which belonged to a Presbyterian Church I attended. I attended church only because I wanted to be in the brigade. I had good times drilling in the basement of that church. I soon became top sergeant and was very proud of my red chevrons. Red, because we were a part of the Artillery —Coast Guard Artillery.

The man who organized this brigade, Major ———, was a queer. He loved boys—and all the parents referred to him as a "lovely man." He loved us a little too much for his own good. Every night, when we reported for duty, he ushered us into his little office, made us sit on his lap, then hugged, squeezed and kissed us as much as he could. We all dreaded these sessions but none of us had the courage to tell on him. No one would have believed us anyway, because he didn't look the part. He was probably bisexual and he probably did love us. One day, however, someone did tell on him, and he was expelled from the church in disgrace. To tell the truth, we felt sorry for him. There were worse buggers in the church than poor Major ——— but they never got caught.

Anyway, this was the sort of activity Jimmy did not take part in. He was probably too busy with school anyway. He had made up his mind to become a lawyer, and he did become one, after a long, hard struggle.

We met rarely now—usually by accident on the street. At each meeting we would exchange views—about God, about politics, about books and about the state of the world. Somehow even at that early stage Jimmy secretly admired me because he sensed the writer in me. About most everything we disagreed, but in a friendly way. I usually ended up telling him that though I didn't believe in politics, if he were to run for office I would vote for him. And I really meant it, though to be honest I never voted

[67]

once in my whole life. Yes, if Jimmy had run for President of the United States I would definitely have voted for him. He was honest, truthful, serious and loyal.

The school we attended was P.S. 85 — on the corner of Covert Street and Evergreen Avenue. We had a school song which we sang on occasion. It began — "Dear 85. . . ." — very sentimental, sloppily so. Even to this day I get a card now and then from Jimmy, reminding me of dear old 85. He is, of course, one of its honored alumni.

But this street, Evergreen Avenue — another one of those Brooklyn Streets which had no character. Not exactly slummy, but poor, run-down, and nondescript. Jimmy's father had his shoe repair shop on it, almost opposite the school. I remember the bakery and the delicatessen store vividly. They were both run by Germans. (Only the druggist was non-German). He was Jewish — and a man I could talk to.) The rest were walking vegetables — turnips, kohlrabi, cauliflower, artichokes. What are called "solid citizens." Somewhere along this avenue was a Baptist Church painted all white. Aside from that I remember nothing. Just sameness, dreariness, shopkeepers, vegetables.

The school I shall always remember, especially for several unusual teachers. Number one was Miss Cordes. "Miss," I say — she may have been fifty or sixty. Whatever she taught — arithmetic, English or what — was only secondary, relatively unimportant. What she really taught us, and that's why we all loved her, was brotherly love — how to look at the world, one's neighbor, and oneself. She emanated joy, peace, confidence — and faith. Not religious faith but faith in life itself. She made one feel that it was good to be alive, that we were *lucky* to be alive. How wonderful! When I think of all the sour pusses we had to put up with, or the sadists, Miss Cordes stands out like a Joan of Arc. I often say I learned nothing at school. But to have been in Miss Cordes' class was a great privilege and worth more than all the knowledge in the world.

Number two was Jack — — — , teacher of the graduating class.

[68]

He was what you might call "a card." I imagine he was either a homosexual or a bisexual. The female teachers adored him. He had a glib tongue, could tell risque stories, and was always in good humor. Unlike Major ——— he made no advances to any of us. At the worst he told us dirty stories. If anything, he seemed to like women. He was very free with them, both in speech and with his hands—and they adored this. I can still see him patting Miss ———'s rump and she giggling like a schoolgirl.

I used to watch him leave school on his way home. He was very dapper, always well dressed, always sporting a bowler and sometimes an ivory-handled cane. We didn't learn very much from him. We enjoyed ourselves in his class—he made us feel as if we were already young men, not fourteen and fifteen-year-old kids.

There were other teachers, also important in my life. Miss M, whom I just mentioned made me aware that even school teachers have sex. With M it wasn't just sex, but cunt. You felt that hers was forever itching, that the thing she craved most was a good lay by Jack wearing a carnation in his buttonhole. You could very easily imagine her cornering him in some dark corner and opening his fly. She had a permanently fixed expression of lust on her face, her lips always slightly parted as if waiting to take it in her mouth. Her laugh was a dirty laugh. She was thoroughly impure, you might say. But attractive. She made the other teachers look sick. She always wore tight-fitting skirts, low-cut blouses which revealed her beautiful boobies, and she used strong perfume, the musky kind which tends to give one a hard-on whether horny or not.

Last but not least was the good, honest Scot, Mr. McDonald. I was quite young when I was in his class, and quite shy and innocent. I remember one day especially when he singled me out as an example to the class. He had been explaining to us via the blackboard some difficult arithmetical problem. When he finished he turned to the class and asked if we all understood now. Everyone nodded in agreement. Except me. I stood up and told him that I didn't understand anything. Whereupon the

[69]

whole class burst into laughter. What a dummy I was! And to stand up and admit it — no, that was too good a joke.

But Mr. McDonald took a different view of it. Holding up his hand he ordered the class to be silent. Then he beckoned me to stand up again. And then he told the class to take a good look at me and try to behave like me. "This Henry Miller has courage," he said. "He's not ashamed to admit he doesn't know. He's genuine, he's sincere. I want you to take an example from him."

Naturally I was flabbergasted. I hadn't given any thought to my behavior — it was just a natural reaction. But I was rather proud of myself nevertheless.

The one person I detested and despised was the principal — Dr. Peewee. To me he was a fop, a show-off and a hypocrite. To begin with he was not my idea of a man. He was frail, flat-chested, and haughty. He gave the illusion of being a great scholar, a know-it-all, but I never understood what he was a doctor in. Every now and then he would invite a Dr. Brown to visit the school and give us students a chance. Evidently Dr. Brown had at one time been a pupil at "dear old 85." Soon as he appeared on the platform the whole auditorium broke into song — "Dear 85, we'll ever strive, to honor thy fair name. . . ." Then Dr. Brown, always freshly returned from his travels abroad, would launch into a speech that might last an hour or two. Always very interesting, I must say. Somewhere along the line he would turn to Dr. Peewee and in his most melting tone of voice tell how he missed dear old 85. Perhaps it was in Singapore or Sierra Leone, or the Engadine — some far-off place none of us knew anything about. Anyhow it all came off perfect — like a good cheese cake. One never asked Dr. Brown what the hell he was doing in these far away places.

Certainly Dr. Peewee and George Wright were two utterly different types of principals. Dr. Peewee never seemed to look a woman in the eyes. Nor did he size up her bottom or her teats. He would pop in and out of a classroom like a lost owl.

He was a frequent visitor at my friend Jack Lawton's home, as was Major — — — , and of course distinguished guests like Dr.

Brown or some cock-eyed Senator or Congressman. The Lawtons were from the old country — England — and very social-minded. My friend Jack at eleven or twelve was already highly sophisticated and of course very well mannered too. I used to like to hear him say — "Sir." "Sir, may I pour you another cup of tea" or some such shit. Which made him a little suspect with the other students. Was he a queer? Was he putting on airs? Where did he think he was getting off? And such like. He proved himself by becoming a first lieutenant in the boy's brigade. He was a great reader for his age. At fourteen he had swallowed all of Dickens and Kipling, and most of Joseph Conrad and Thomas Hardy. He didn't have to work, I mean, study diligently, like most of us. Everything came easy to him, it seemed. He also was lucky to have a loving, devoted mother. He didn't think much of Jimmy Pasta. Referred to him as a climber and a peasant at heart. Naturally one could not possibly think of Dr. Peewee visiting Jimmy's home, in the back of the cobbler's shop. Mrs. Pasta wouldn't have understood a word Dr. Peewee said. Nor would Mr. Pasta, it goes without saying.

Only a short distance up the street, or avenue, was the German delicatessen shop as I said. I can see myself dropping in there every Sunday evening to buy the same things for our Sunday meal. Pot cheese with rich cream on it, salami, liverwurst, head cheese, potato salad, blutwurst, and a variety of bolognas that were very tasty. Then a dash to the bakery across the street where I either got an apple cake or a streusel kuchen. This was our Sunday meal come rain or shine. And I never tired of it.

But what I could never get over were the proprietors of these shops. Both places run by women, fat, bloated, ignorant, illiterate, narrow-minded, money mad. Never once did I hear an intelligent conversation between them and any of their customers. I used to be furious. Just looking at them gave me the creeps. Long before the rise of Hitler I was anti-German. Later I discovered that these German-Americans were worse than the Germans themselves, that is to say, more stupid, more swinish,

[71]

more mean and money grubbing. More vegetable like.

The years passed and Jimmy still had his nose to the grind-stone and one eye always open to publicity. While Jimmy is busy studying to get his degree in law and from there work his way up to being a Congressman, I was busy living my chaotic get-nowhere life.

I had finally disengaged myself from the widow, by telling her I had gone to Juneau, Alaska. I was just twenty-one. I never got to Alaska, nor did I become a cowboy as I had hoped. But I held a number of jobs on ranches. Then one day I ran into Emma Goldman, the anarchist, in San Diego and from there on the whole course of my life changed. That is, instead of staying out West I decided to return to New York and become an intellec-tual. It was her lectures on Nietzsche and other famous European authors which made me change direction. Of course the widow also had something to do with my return. I found that I missed her, especially the good fucks we had. Finally, however, I did ditch her. By now I had become acquainted with the woman who was to become my first wife. She was my piano teacher. I knew her only a few months before marrying her. We quarreled almost from the very beginning. Sometimes we rolled on the floor struggling with one another. It was truly disgraceful the life we led.

One night I passed a cinema and suddenly decided to go in. Who meets me at the door with a flashlight but the widow. She was an usher there. I forgot to say that in disappearing from her sight the second time I had given her some cock and bull story. The moment I stepped inside the theatre she burst into tears. She was still weeping as she escorted me to a seat and sat down beside me. "Harry, Harry," she said softly, "how could you do that to me?" And then she sobbed and wept some more. I waited for her to go off duty, then escorted her home.

Naturally the first thing that happened as we entered her flat was to love it up. Before you could say Jack Robinson she had whisked off her dress and was lying on the kitchen table, waiting for me to slip it in. And, as we began to fuck she began to weep again. As everyone knows, there is no more enjoyable fuck to be had than from a woman in tears. When we had finished I listened to her woes, to all the misfortunes which had befallen her since we parted. I was truly sorry for her. As I walked home I hit upon an idea which I thought would solve the problem. I would tell my wife the whole story and ask her to let me bring the widow to live with us. Why couldn't the three of us live together in peace and harmony? The Mormons were able to do it, often with many wives. And I had no intention of marrying the widow, only of taking her in as a friend.

Of course when I broached the idea to my wife she hit the ceiling. She said I must be mad to even entertain such an idea. I suppose any woman would agree with her.

But the odd thing about it all was that I was serious. Serious and innocent. But I was the only one who saw it that way. I was too ashamed ever to go back and see the widow again. Pauline was her name. She was a good woman, had no vices, and asked for but little. Through me fate dealt her a cruel blow. Certainly she would have made me a better wife than my first one did.

During this period I went from one job to another, never lasting very long in any of them. One of the better jobs I got through a customer of my father's. Grant was his name. He was a vice-president, I believe, of the Federal Reserve Bank in the Wall Street district. I was given a job, along with about thirty other men and women, checking the adding machines for errors. A boring job, but the pay was good and my fellow workers a jolly bunch. I was on the job about two months, everything going well when one day I was asked to go see the personnel manager. To my great surprise he told me he was discharging me. Why? I wanted to know. Wasn't my work satisfactory?

Oh, there was nothing wrong with my work, he hastened to assure me. It was my character.

"My character?" I exclaimed.

"Yes," he said. "We have been investigating your life, interrogating your friends and neighbors—we know quite a bit about you."

[73]

And then he told me how they had discovered about me and the widow.

"We are not questioning your morals," he went on. "but we feel we can't trust you."

He then went on to tell me to my face that because of this obvious infatuation for an older woman, there was no telling what I might do.

I was enraged. "What is it I might do that would hurt the bank?" I wanted to know.

"Rob it!" he said blandly.

"No, you don't mean that," I said. "Why it's preposterous."

He didn't think so. There was no way of talking him out of it. I was finished, no question about it.

And so it went from job to job. Until finally I managed to put in four years as employment manager of the messenger department in the telegraph company. It was toward the end of this period I met June at the dance hall. A few months later I quit my job in the Western Union, having decided to risk all in becoming a writer. It was now my real misery began. What I had been through before was only a preparation for what was to follow.

In quitting the Western Union I had promised June I would not take another job. I was to stay home and write and she would take care of things. It didn't work out as planned, not that we were not diligent, but luck was against us. I did a lot of writing which never appeared in print. Finally I wrote under *her* name — June Mansfield — and thus had a bit of success. But it was short-lived.

Then came Jean — a strange beautiful creature whom June took a fancy to. They behaved like a pair of Lesbians. After a couple of months they began talking of going to Europe together. Jean was a painter, a poet and sculptress. She also made puppets. She made one they christened "Count Bruga," which caused a sensation wherever they appeared.

It was about this time that I took to panhandling at night on Broadway. Even that was a failure. Night after night I came

[74]

home empty-handed. We were living like savages now in the basement of an apartment house. The rooms we occupied had once been a laundry. It was a cold winter and I had chopped all the furniture to pieces to make firewood. To me it seemed like the dead end. How much lower could we sink?

One day toward dinner hour, I am wandering slowly back to the house. I am not merely depressed, I am dejected. Besides I am starved. I don't recall when we had a last good meal.

All of a sudden whom do I run into but Jimmy Pasta. He is now an Assemblyman from his district. Looks keen and prosperous. Cordial greetings.

"Well, Hen, old boy, how are you doing?" says Jimmy, giving me a slap on the back.

For answer I say — "Rotten."

Immediately a genuine look of concern came over his countenance.

"What do you mean?" says Jimmy.

"I mean I'm broke. I have no job, and I'm hungry."

The moment I said hungry his face lit up. "If that's all it is we can fix that right away," he said, and taking me by the arm he led me to a plush bar where he was known and ordered a meal for me.

"Tell me all about it," he says, as we sat down. "What's happened to you? The last time I heard about you you were the editor of some magazine."

I gave him a wry smile. "I was the assistant editor of a catalog for the Charles Williams Mail Order House. No literature connected with that job," I added.

Well, we sat and talked. I had a few beers, we spoke of "dear old 85" and so on. Finally I said — "I need a job, Jimmy. I need it bad. Could you help me?"

I knew he was secretary to the Park Commissioner — a cushy job that probably paid well.

To my surprise Jimmy replied that he could fix me up with a job in his own office.

[75]

"I may have to put you on the payroll as a grave digger first," said Jimmy. "Do you mind?"

"Hell, no," I said. "I've been a ditch digger, a garbage collector and what not. Just so long as I get a salary."

When I left Jimmy I went home sailing. I had agreed to be at his office at nine in the morning next day. He would introduce me to the Commissioner himself—a big-wig now in the political world.

June and Jean took the good news rather unenthusiastically, I thought. They were curious to know what my salary would be.

Next day I went, met the Commissioner, and was immediately put on the payroll. For the first week or so I might be obliged to dig graves but after that I would be made Jimmy's assistant. It sounded wonderful to me.

The next morning I was up bright and early to tackle my new job. It didn't take me long to catch on. The other workers were friendly and helpful. Two of them were from the old 14th Ward. That made things still nicer.

On the way home that evening I stopped off at a florist to buy some flowers.

"A nice touch for a change," I thought. I rang the door bell. No answer. No lights either. In order to get in I had to ring the landlady's bell.

I entered our joint in the dark, lit a candle or two—the electricity had long been shut off. On the floor, in a corner, were a few pieces of discarded clothing. I roamed up and down several times before I noticed a note on my desk. I picked it up and read—"Dear Val, we left for Paris on the Rochambeau this morning. Love. June."

In another book I have described the emotion that overcame me and my feeling of desolation.

"No wonder," I thought to myself that they showed such little enthusiasm when I told them of the job. What they really felt was a feeling of relief, that someone was looking after me. It made them less guilty.

Next day I told Jimmy what had happened. He could read the
sad news on my face.

"You say you love her?" he asked.

I nodded.

"Maybe I'm lucky then," he said. "I haven't met anyone so
far who could play such tricks on me."

It was true. Jimmy had little time for women. He was completely involved now in politics. He aimed to go to Washington
in a year or two.

Sometimes he invited me to have lunch with him — usually at
a bar in the back room of which the local politicians met, played
cards, drank like fish and so on. More and more he was becoming disillusioned with the racket. He even went so far as to
say there were no honest politicians — impossible.

When I inquired what kept him from behaving like the others
he replied very simply — "Because I'm different. Because I have
ideals. Lincoln was no crook. Neither was Thomas Jefferson. I
wouldn't bring disgrace on my mother and father's name . . .
Remember, Hen, old 85? Remember Miss Cordes? Maybe she's
helped a lot to keep me straight."

To his credit I must say that Jimmy never did waver. That's
why perhaps he never got very far. But everyone respected him.
He was still written up in the local papers — as something of "a
white hope." He still gave lectures to Boy Scouts and other groups
of youngsters. He talked as if he actually *were* President.

It was only three or four days after the two of them had sailed
that I received a Radiogram from the ship. It said, "Please
cable fifty dollars before we dock. Desperate. June."

Once again I had to face Jimmy. I felt terribly ashamed and
humiliated. He lent me the money, not without a little ser-
mon and a monologue about what fools men can be.

Myself, I couldn't understand why they needed this sum.
Could they be in debt already? I knew that once they reached
Paris they would be o.k. June had the faculty of making people
believe in her and trust in her.

[77]

Meanwhile I would pay Jimmy back so much a week out of my salary. I had gone back to the folk's house to live — it was cheaper. Almost every day I sat at a little desk they had given me as a child and I wrote to June.

Every Saturday afternoon found me at a dance hall on Broadway. In one afternoon I would spend a week's pin money. But I enjoyed it. Besides I needed to relax and to get a good fuck, even if it were only a dry fuck. Most of these taxi dance girls were very good looking and hot in the pants. They enjoyed these blind fucks on the dance floor — their only concern was not to have their dresses soiled by the man's sperm. I think I have already mentioned how I would take them to another kind of dance hall on their day off. And give them a stand-up fuck in the hallway when I took them home. One girl used to take me to her home and squat over me while I sat on a chair in the kitchen in the dark. Sometimes her mother passed through the room while we were at it but she was unaware of our doings because she was stone deaf and almost totally blind. This particular bitch seemed to enjoy it all the more when her mother passed through the room. She could come easily and it always seemed to me that she came during these critical moments.

Meanwhile I was getting letters from June. They weren't finding it very easy to get along in Paris, but fortunately she had made a great friend of the famous sculptor Ossip Zadkine. She might just as well have said Picasso. Zadkine was world famous. Some years later when I myself went to Paris he asked me what had become of the paintings and pieces of sculpture he had given June to sell in America. June must have disposed of them without telling me. From the brief conversation I had with him and from a few slips June made herself it wasn't difficult to deduct that they had a merry time of it together, punctuated by occasional trips to the Bois de Boulogne where, like Hyde Park, London, any and everyone lay on the grass and fucked whomever they pleased.

Working as Jimmy's assistant I grew more and more familiar with Jimmy's life. Part of his job was to write the political speeches his boss, the Commissioner, had to make. Now and then he would ask my aid in phrasing a sentence. He seemed to regard me as a full-fledged writer. I was in fear he would one day ask *me* to write the speeches for him.

Best time was lunch time at the bar, when he would pour out his heart to me. He really hated the life his brother politicians lived and some of which he had to share. There was never any mention of women. Only card playing, gambling, pool and guzzling. He was with them but not of them.

Somehow it was only now that I began to warm up to him, to discover what a good, loyal friend he was. He had all the sterling qualities which a politician seldom has. As I said before, this was probably his handicap. He never got to Washington. He remained a local Congressman. I never heard much from him or about him once I quit the Park Department job. Occasionally, I would receive a postcard from him. I still do. And I always answer immediately. For I regard Jimmy as one of the few genuine friends in my life, one of the several men who saved my life.

But perhaps what I am most indebted to Jimmy for is this. One afternoon, thinking about Jean and June in Paris, and all the ups and downs in my life, I decided to outline the events in my life from the beginning. I sat down to type out this outline, which in fact became the synopsis for all my autobiographical romances. I sat down at closing time one afternoon and I remained there typing till about five o'clock next morning. In the space of about thirty pages I managed to recall most everything of importance in my life to date. And all without effort. It was as if I had turned on some tap in my memory and the images just flowed out. It was with this outline that I began writing my autobiography in Paris. Not immediately, to be sure. I first wrote a couple of novels in which I used the third person.

As I say, about five in the morning I was pooped. I lay down on the rug in the Commissioner's office and fell asleep. Around eight a.m. the first worker arrived. He saw me lying on the rug and I thought was dead, thought I had committed suicide.

Now that I have told the story of our friendship I must send Jimmy a card to wish him well. He has read my books but I never told him that they were really born in his office.

A view of Driggs Avenue, the street I lived on the first nine years of my life.

CHAPTER FIVE

Joe O'Reagan

Joe came into my life out of nowhere.

All his life he was dropping in on me—from nowhere, it seemed. He was a born wanderer, of a buoyant, optimistic disposition and possessed of great (Irish) charm. He was attractive to women, with his blarney, his black, curly locks, his violet eyes and long eye lashes, plus his way of throwing himself on their mercy.

As a boy of five he and his older brother had been put in an orphan asylum, a Catholic one, by his Irish mother and her second husband, a Russian Jew. Joe had never forgiven either of them for this. At the age of ten he and his brother managed to escape from the asylum. The brother later became a sheriff somewhere in Texas.

Evidently Joe hadn't received much of an education at the orphan asylum. He had a perpetual itch for knowledge and culture. On the other hand he was rather precocious. For example, he had diddled the Mother Superior, who apparently was

[81]

very fond of him. He did it cunningly and cold-bloodedly.

I said that women found him attractive — perhaps because he had a perpetual hard-on. As for men, no, they were not taken in by his Irish charm, his cunning and his boasting. At first blush he seemed to inspire distrust. As my friends often remarked — "There's something fishy about him." What Joe was looking for was a mother's love, or at least confidence in his good faith. He needed people to believe in him, trust him.

When he ran away from the asylum he joined a circus and shortly thereafter met a man, a zoologist, I believe, who took a great interest in him. Through this man he learned to love all God's creatures, including snakes. Animals belonged to his world — he understood them.

When I say he came from nowhere I mean he lacked the usual, ordinary background most of us possessed. He knew a little about everything and nothing much of anything. He read a great deal and was very responsive to books and authors. He had his idols, as did Stanley and I. He could talk well — the gift of gab, as we say.

I came across Joe, oddly enough, about ten o'clock at night in a New Jersey village where my folks were spending their summer vacation. They had chosen the place because of the lake — Swartswood Lake — which offered swimming, boating and fishing.

I had taken with me, for a few days, a friend of our neighborhood, a fellow my own age, named Bill Woodruff. Joe and he worked together in a maintenance and repair shop run by an eccentric bachelor who was interested in young men. Bill Woodruff was somewhat of a sissy or "molly-coddle" as we called it then, a spoiled brat, a weakling, and in no sense of the word manly or robust. Anyway, he kept telling me about this O'Reagan chap and thought I should meet him. And so, one night, as we were standing on the road, along comes a horse and carriage, and who jumps out to greet us but Joe O'Reagan. I liked Joe immediately. I liked his voice and his handshake. He struck me as not only handsome but very manly.

[82]

In a few minutes we were at the lake in a rowboat. It was pitch dark. Suddenly I hear a splash and it is O'Reagan who has dived into the middle of the lake. He takes an eternity to surface. "I was caught in the bullrushes," he explained, laughing it off as if it were nothing. Woodruff was terrified. He didn't know how to swim and was frightened of the water. But Joe was like a water snake.

Then and there we sealed a pact of friendship. It lasted till Joe's death a few years ago.

As I said earlier, Joe was always coming and going — destination unknown. He followed his hunches. Just before we met he had been released from the Army, where he had worked his way up from private to top-sergeant. It was a treat to hear him talk about the abilities needed to be a good top-sergeant. To hear him talk, a top-sergeant, a good one, that is, was more important than a general.

In a way the Army furnished him with some sort of education. He had gone to the Far East — to China, Indo-China, Java and Japan. In Japan he discovered the Japanese woman. He never ceased admiring her. One of the things he liked to dwell on was the cleanliness of the Japanese — even in their whorehouses. To hear him, the whorehouse procedure was a ceremony of the highest order. The girl not only bathed herself scrupulously, but the man too. Then came the exquisite kimonos, the cup of tea, the samisen, flowers, birds in their cages. Not even Count Keyserling, who devoted some of his best pages to Japan on the Japanese woman, told it better than Joe. It was then and there I really began dreaming of the Orient, and of Japan especially. (Of course Joe had greatly exaggerated and improvised, as I learned later, but what matter?)

Wherever he had been he could discourse on it like a poet. I often wondered that he had never tried to write. I could listen to him, rapt, for hours at a time. What a treat to hear about such little-known parts of the world, to learn of the delicacy, the finesse of these people.

[83]

It took me some time before I discovered that people didn't think as highly as I did of Joe. As I remarked before, most of my friends were distrustful and suspicious of him. Joe was always promoting somebody or something. (For a good part of his life it was me and my work.) He went about it, unfortunately, as if he were stalking big game.

Women regarded him quite differently from men. They usually adored him and melted under his blandishments. With them he acted the abandoned child, the misunderstood and unappreciated young man of the world. He didn't have to sell women — they took to him immediately. Being sly with his hands, Joe usually made his women fast. Often he let them keep him. Not that he was a sponger. No, Joe was generous at heart. But he was often broke. When things got too bad he would up and leave — it didn't matter where to — he simply had to find other air to breathe.

Every time he came home to roost it was *chez moi*. Joe liked the way I lived and the women I was in love with. He would often implore me to allow him to share a woman with him. He saw nothing wrong with that. He would tell me that I was "lucky."

At the same time he would take it upon himself to defend me, protect me. He couldn't understand how a "great writer" such as myself could go unnoticed. He read everything I wrote, not once, but several times. He talked of my pieces as if he had written them himself.

Evenings, when he returned from his self-imposed campaigns, he would relate in detail what had happened in the course of his interviews with editors, publishers and critics. He was always promising me quick results, great results. But somehow everything always fell through at the last minute. This hurt Joe more than I. I was getting habituated to rejection slips. Perhaps I bolstered my courage by pretending to myself that I was America's greatest writer, the logical descendant of Walt Whitman. Certainly everything I wrote seemed like pure gold to me. I compared my work only to the foremost writers — Petronius,

Rabelais, Emerson, Whitman. I considered myself superior to such as Sinclair Lewis, Theodore Dreiser, Sherwood Anderson, Ben Hecht, et alia. I was unique — in a class by myself.

And so, when Joe was deflated, I would comfort *him*.

I don't remember ever quarreling with him. Discussion and argument we had aplenty. We spent interminable hours bandying words about every subject under the sun. For Joe, if uneducated, was highly intelligent. Moreover, he questioned everything. He had been raised a Catholic in the orphan asylum but had ceased to believe in it long before leaving the asylum. The only thing he liked about the nuns, for example, was that they were so naive. To Joe they were all pushovers, including the Mother Superior, who wore a truss. It was like listening to the "Decameron" to hear Joe tell about the nuns and their craving for a bit of nooky.

When I became employment manager of the telegraph company I made Joe my assistant. He thoroughly enjoyed the work. It gave him pleasure, for example, to spot a crook or an epileptic. Frequently he would slip me a note while I was interviewing an applicant, warning me that the guy I was talking to was a bad egg or urging me to observe the scars on the man's hand or arm. (A sign that he was an epileptic and had suffered many falls.)

We sat opposite each other at the same desk. It amused me to see how seriously he took the job. What a thing he made of it! As if he were the president of the company.

In the office we had two beautiful young women; he took one and I took the other. The two girls lived together, which made it easier for us. At this time I was still married.

It often happened that I repaired to the couch for a snooze after dinner. I was usually pooped because during all the time I served the telegraph company I never got enough sleep. It was always two or three a.m. before I got to bed. And I was supposed to be at my office at eight o'clock a.m. (Naturally I was always late, often unshaved, often appearing in a blue denim shirt frayed at the collar and sleeves.)

[85]

When I lay down to take my nap my wife would first sit down in a rocker near the coach, waiting for me to invite her to lie beside me. But most of the time I would fall sound asleep. Then my good friend Joe got in some good licks. Pretending to feel sorry for my wife he would soon have her on his lap, and no doubt massaging her cunt while I snored blissfully away. But things always worked out to my advantage somehow. After Joe had warmed her up she would slip over to the couch, and, without waking me, would put her hand in my fly and play with my prick and balls. Naturally, I would soon open my eyes. Then I would commence to give her a going over. She was a very passionate, if inhibited creature. (She too had been brought up as a Catholic, in a convent.) Later, when I knew her better, I suspected that some of her "dear friends," as she called them, were out and out Lesbians. But this did not prevent her from being a good lay. And so, as a reward, Joe was allowed to sit in the rocking chair and watch us make love. I can still see him putting his hands to his ears to shut out the groans and grunts we made.

Joe had lived with me during the period I was with the widow. We were all frightfully poor then, kept alive, you might say, by our boarder, a streetcar motorman. On the pittance he doled out to us from his weekly salary, we managed to eat round steak and boiled potatoes at least three times a week. Never a dessert. Never a good drink—of wine, gin or whiskey. We lived like hermits and fucked like rabbits. There was nothing else to do. The money Joe put on the table when he arrived was soon gone. Perhaps we managed to see a movie a few times—Clara Bow, Charlie Chaplin, Charles Ray—or Alice Joyce. As there seemed no hope of getting a job, we slept late. Joe would sometimes crawl into bed with us and try his best to get his end in. He always pleaded like a man who had been terribly deprived. How could we let him suffer like that, was his attitude.

If I were absent of an afternoon he would be sure to make advances to her. I would sometimes come home to find her in tears. What was the matter? *Joe.* She liked Joe, but she deeply resented

[86]

his making advances to her. (We regarded ourselves as good as married then.) Later I was actually going to get married to her, but my mother had come at me with a cleaver, threatening to kill me if I ever said another word about marriage!

The motorman, Tex was his name, was a *"gentleman."* He would never dream of doing anything behind my back. (He was from Texas.)

This business of Joe coming to live with me (or us) continued into my next marriage. But with Mona he didn't dare make any overtures. Mona impressed him from the first. The two had something in common — extreme generosity and a flair for exaggeration. I used to listen to them as if I were observing a stage performance. Both were wonderful liars and both believed their own lies.

What hurt Joe, what he found difficult to believe, was that even by this time I was still in the soup. I had not as yet sold a thing. (I had had a short article — my first! — accepted and published in a magazine for Negroes, but had received no money for it.) Joe wanted to rectify all this. How could the world ignore his great friend and great writer, Henry Miller? But the world did, and not even a Joe O'Reagan, with all his charm, bluster and blarney, could prevail. The time was not ripe. Somehow I understood it and accepted it patiently and impatiently.

I cursed not only editors and publishers but the public too. I scorned their heroes, their idols. I cursed every mother's son for the stupid, insensitive bastard that he was. (I still do in my better moments.) The picture has not changed since those days. I was lucky, that's all. I have a wonderful Jupiter.

One of the things I never told Joe was that I was fucking his girl friend on the side. I didn't do it out of revenge or to teach him a lesson. It just happened. She had been married to one of my very best friends, a young man I admired and regarded as a genius.

Anyway, the two of them never got along very well, and I soon got to know his wife intimately. I made the mistake of introducing her to O'Reagan, who was quick to nibble at the bait.

[87]

For a while we were both screwing her. But then there was the other girl in the office — funny, I can't remember her name anymore — and I was content to leave Elsa to Joe.

We did a lot of fucking in those days, especially after the telegraph company decided to hire women as messengers. Now Joe could no longer complain. He was swamped with lays. Everything ended in cunt, it seemed. I often tend to forget this glorious period, being so pissed off by my failure to make it as a writer.

Though cunt was in the air and we were getting our fill, I was madly in love with my second wife. It sounds crazy, but I never felt that I betrayed her. To fuck someone else was not necessarily an act of betrayal. It was a sign of life, the celebration of life.

When I left for Europe in 1930 I didn't see O'Reagan again until some time after my return. I don't recall now what he was doing for a living then, but it must certainly have been promotional work or public relations. He hadn't changed a bit — the same bluster, same blarney, same empty rhetoric. The only good thing about him was his taste in literature. We would sit up till all hours of the night talking of our favorite writers and favorite characters. By now he had read most of Dostoievsky and the other great Russians. I introduced him to Berdyaev. He had also digested Thomas Mann, Gide, Proust and much of Balzac. He spoke as if with authority. I didn't dare contradict him. As for me, my work, well he had faithfully followed my career, had read everything I wrote, and knew what the critics thought of me.

It must have been after the "Air-Conditioned Nightmare" trip that I ran into Joe — at some bar on Third Avenue. I was happy to tell him about the old friends I had looked up during that trip. I was particularly eager to tell him about the Colonel and the General I had met. They had grown up with me — lived only a few doors away from us. One was about seven years older than I, the other (the General) about four years older. They still treated me as if I were a little boy. Naturally, they had never cracked a book of mine. They simply didn't read. Mostly they played cards, swapped stories with fellow officers and guzzled tons of beer. Thoroughly uninteresting characters, both of them. I reminded Joe of what he had told me about top sergeants. Though I have never had any traffic with them I could believe what Joe had said, that without them the Army couldn't get along.

The thing about the General was that as a boy or young man I had thought him effeminate. Now that he was a general he was still effeminate-looking to me. His brother, the Colonel, on the other hand, was a whore monger. Every other word he uttered was a curse word.

Later in life I had occasion to meet other officers of the Army, Navy and Marines. Of them all I can say that they seemed to have only two things on their mind — cunt and booze.

Yes, later in life I had occasion to meet what might be considered the cream of our society. I must confess I never met one officer for whom I had the least respect; I met only two college professors for whom I had any respect; I never met a great business executive for whom I had the least respect. I did meet now and then a priest or a monk with whom I could converse intelligently, laugh heartily and discuss spiritual matters with enjoyment. I say a priest or/and a monk. Never a Protestant minister, a Rabbi once.

On this trip I had also stopped off to see a buddy from high school days. He was now a professor of music in a girl's college somewhere in South Carolina. Another disappointment. He might just as well have been a professor of zoology or paleontology. Yet at fifteen he was a marvelous pianist, someone obviously destined for the concert stage.

This time Joe didn't ask me to put him up. I was on the go myself — and besides, he now had a job and a woman (not his wife) who was devoted to him. He had become quite a respectable citizen. Still a great boozer, still a bamboozler, but toned down now, two feet on the ground. I inquired about his sister. Apparently she had married. He said it mournfully. I recalled

[89]

the look on his face when he first introduced her to me. She was indeed a beauty — an Irish beauty — and it seemed obvious that he not only loved her as a sister but that he was in love with her.

Knowing what a disreputable bastard he was, I often wondered why he didn't fuck his own sister. *I* would have, had I been in his place. But Joe did have certain scruples after all. Though he always referred to his mother as a dirty Irish bitch it was obvious that he loved her dearly. His hatred for her husband was based not only on the fact that he was a stepfather and a Russian Jew to boot but that he had robbed Joe of his rightful place — as her lover.

When we talked of these things Joe would come out with some rather surprising reminiscences. One was about his attempt to screw a cow. He had screwed sheep a number of times and maybe mares (Shetland ponies) too, for all I know. He was capable of screwing a snake, if it could be managed. I wondered why he had never fallen in love with a Japanese or Filipino girl. "Lack of money," he always replied. By that he meant that were he to find one such he would feel obliged to treat her like a queen. American girls were to him just cunts, at the best "broads." He despised the Average American Girl. The English, of course, were beneath attention.

It never occurred to either of us in those days that I would one day marry a Japanese woman. As for Chinese women, one never encountered any anywhere. The only Chinese we knew were the laundry man and the waiters in chop suey joints.

Joe was not much of a correspondent, nor did he telephone often. Usually he just dropped in — from God knows where. He *could* write, however. Only his letters were all alike. He wrote the same sort of letter whether telling me about Dostoievsky, deep-sea fishing, golf, a new sales campaign, or the art and elegance of the Japanese woman. To me, knowing him as I did, it was incredible. It was as if he had been put through some correspondence school as a kid, been thoroughly brainwashed, and given 100% on his exams. It's been my great misfortune that for most

[90]

my life *I* had to be the letter writer. Whether I wrote to a man friend or a woman I was deeply in love with, the responses were usually tardy and never what I expected. Which only led me to write more letters. The true letter writer seems to be a thing of the past. To be honest, those famous letter writers are not my favorites.

But as regards Joe — if he wasn't much of a letter writer he was, on the other hand, a great storyteller. And here is another thing which baffles me — the natural born storyteller may be totally unable to write a simple tale, or a decent letter, for that matter. He may not know how to spell, his grammar may be nil, his imagination paralyzed, but he can hold you spell-bound once he starts to spout. Whereas I have often noticed that good writers may not have the ability to tell a good story at all. Well, Joe was a natural born storyteller. He told fantastic yarns. He worked in all the details, just as do certain classic composers who bore the shit out of me. For some strange reason, in a story these details are exciting, heighten one's interest, and so on. Also, should you happen to question a certain detail, let us say, that leads the storyteller off on a detour which can be utterly fascinating. Of course the ideal storyteller demands the ideal listener. I regard myself as an ideal listener. I am a sucker for anyone who has something to get off his chest. That endears me to many people. They think I am sincerely interested in what they are telling me. Often I am not, but I listen attentively just the same.

Sometimes, while listening to such people, I am thinking what *I* might do with such a story, or I interpolate silently where there are gaps in the tale. Or I get lost, thinking of the corrections in grammar I am making. Or again, his story may remind me of one I had intended to write long ago, and I am feverishly making mental notes — brief, telegraphic messages — which will help me to remember when he's through.

With Joe it was possible to play games. I could interrupt him at any time, I could question his veracity. I could tell him what his story reminded me of — frequently, even an untalented in-

[91]

dividual like Joe could hit on a theme already exploited by saying a Maupassant, a Flaubert, a Gogol, or to come down a bit, by a Jack London or an O'Henry. In a way, this storytelling of his took his mind off cunt. He never told dirty stories. He would like to have talked, he told me, like Joseph Conrad wrote. The strange thing is, Irish that he was, he had never read Shaw nor O'Casey. He liked Oscar Wilde and the man who translated *Tristan and Yseult*. He adored Lewis Carroll but couldn't abide Shakespeare. (He preferred Marlowe.)

All in all, he was a strange mixture of things. Very much like myself. Perhaps that's why we got along so well. I don't recall ever quarreling with him. Nor did it bother him that I never introduced him to my other friends. (I had told him in the beginning that my friends didn't take to him very kindly.) It didn't seem to bother him. He simply shrugged his shoulders and put them down as fools and imbeciles. Sometimes he would say — I don't see what you see in so-and-so." "Don't try," I would reply. Or, now and then, if we happened to run into a nut in the street or in a coffee shop, he would say — "I hope you'll put him in your next book. He's pure gold." And usually he was right. Writers don't get much nourishment from other contemporary writers or professors, or intellectuals; their material usually comes from the gutter, from the potentially insane or criminal.

Up to the end, which was only a few years ago, O'Reagan's letters always ended with his telling me in what bully condition he was. (He died in his early seventies.) Yes, his bowels moved perfectly, he had no trouble pissing, could fuck like a stallion, drink all the booze he wanted, and so on. And, so, when I got the news of his death, I was surprised rather than shocked. I had expected him to live to be a hundred at least. Like millions of other poor bastards in this fucking land of "the free and the brave," he died of a heart attack — in a bar on Third Avenue.

Considering the efforts he put forth to survive, to find his place in the sun, he should have died twenty years earlier.

I don't know what it takes to survive in this bloody country.

One must have the morals of a stoat, the aggressiveness of a pug, the ruthlessness of an assassin, and the heartlessness of a big magnate — *plus* a barrel of luck! Joe was an ornery bugger, but he was a cavalier compared to the guys in the swim today. Though he had no use for the Pope or the Church, he might, under different circumstances, have made a good Irish priest. All he lacked was their stupidity and bigotry.

épreuve d'artiste — Good news — Henry Miller 1973

Public School No. 17. The elementary school I attended on North 5th Street and Driggs Avenue.

CHAPTER SIX

Max Winthrop

Why there was ever a strong bond between us is a mystery to me now. In many ways we resembled one another, so much so that we were often taken for brothers. In a way, we were both clowns, both ham actors. And, of all those with whom we associated we two possessed the most verve, the most vitality.

We met in high school. Out of nostalgia I had chosen to go to a school in the old neighborhood. And Max was from Greenpoint, not far from my old home in the 14th Ward.

One thing we had in common was our ability to play the piano. He was more adept at it than I, but I was more serious about it. In the famous Xerxes Society which we formed all the members could play *some* instrument.

In school he and I, together with a perhaps a dozen other gentiles, were an enclave in the midst of a completely Jewish population. The teachers, all gentiles and all rather eccentric,

[95]

naturally favored us with good marks. There was no open conflict between the Jews and the gentiles, but we definitely did not mix. And it very obviously rankled us when the Jewish boys showed their superiority in athletics. At handball they were wizards. It seemed as if the game was meant for them. We who were gentile never visited the homes of any of the Jewish boys. Naturally, the boy who carried off scholastic honors was a Jewish boy, a very shy, introverted type, whom we did everything possible to embarrass and humiliate. I said "naturally" he came off first, because we gentiles took our studies lightly whereas the Jewish boys studied like fiends.

It was in the third year in high school that I fell madly in love with Cora Seward who, alas for me, lived nearer to Max than to me. Max saw her frequently and treated her rather nonchalantly, I thought. Which meant to me that he was not in love with her. Max was not in love with any girl. All he had on his mind was cunt, and it was a failing, if you like, which was to last his whole lifetime. All my friends, both in and out of school, knew that I was infatuated with Cora. They all felt sorry for me for being so deeply in love with her. How ironic! As if the supreme gift were not love. Statistically all my friends were "in love," if one could call it that. They all had girlfriends who they called on regularly or brought to the parties we held. Most of them (my friends, I mean) were still virgins. Whereas they saw their girls at regular intervals I saw Cora rarely, only at parties. To dance with her was a great privilege. I trembled all over when I held her in my arms. At these parties we played innocent games like "Kiss the Pillow" and "Post Office." Somehow we had a good time without much drinking. Perhaps a bowl of punch served to take care of all our needs.

As I have related elsewhere at length it was my custom on finishing the evening meal to put on my hat and coat and go for a walk. It was the same walk night after night — a long, long walk to Cora's house on Devoe Street and then home. I never stopped to ring her door bell and have a chat with her. I was content to merely walk slowly past her home in the hope of seeing her shadow in the parlor window. I never did, not once in the three or four years during which I performed this crazy ritual. It finally came to an end when I met the widow and began fucking my head off. Not that I ceased to love Cora. Ah no! I thought of her even when in the midst of fucking the widow. She was on my mind night and day without let. This is what is called "first love" and in the eyes of most people is a sort of puppy love. How woefully ignorant people are, how envious of true love. I have often said, and I repeat it now, that on my dying bed, Cora will probably be the last one I shall think of. I may die with her name on my lips. (On the other hand, if she is still alive and I should chance to run into her one day, what a calamity!)

Max made it his business to keep me informed of Cora's doings. His wife had become friends with Cora, it seems, though what these two had in common, I could never understand. Of course to Max my love for Cora was like a sickness. To him I was an uncurable romantic. As I said before, all he had on his mind was cunt. No wonder he later became a gynecologist. Though to tell the truth, he soon found it a disillusioning profession. As he would say to me confidentially now and then—"There's nothing more disgusting than to be examining cunts all day." Even so, it did not prevent him from fucking everything in sight. Sometimes he thought he would switch to becoming a psychologist or a psychiatrist. He declared that women's ailments were a simple problem—all they needed was to be properly fucked. In the course of time he attracted quite a few well-known figures from the theatrical world. He would give me intimate details about their love life or sex life or and about the kind of cunt they had. It was no trouble giving them a lay. They all seemed to be grateful to him for his attentions. Clever as he was, he now and then got into trouble, but somehow always managed to squirm out of it. I find it interesting to observe that what was then regarded as malpractice is now advocated as excellent therapy by some analysts. The question of therapy aside, there is no denying the fact that a

[97]

woman who is screwed often and expertly is a happy creature. The woman who hums or sings under her breath as she goes about her chores has more than likely been well fucked that day.

At twenty-one Max fell violently ill with pneumonia and probably would have died had it not been for his mother's loving care. When he was well out of danger his parents decided to send him to the farm of a relative where he could fully recuperate. I got permission from my father, for whom I was then working, to spend a week or ten days with Max. I have described this episode in full in *Plexus* and so will not repeat it here. The point is that it is almost impossible to believe that two grown-up men such as we two could behave like children. Rarely have I enjoyed myself as much as during that week at his uncle's farm somewhere in New Jersey. Even there, a total stranger, he soon discovered a young girl whom he used to meet under the bridge after dark and screw.

He wasn't a mime, Max, but he was definitely some kind of actor. He knew how to keep a straight face. Also, he gave the impression that he spoke with authority. At the same time he was an out and out sentimentalist. We who were so often taken for brothers were so very, very, different. Even then, when we were close friends, I despised some of the things he believed in or championed. He always predicted a hard life for me, and of course he was right. But that was one of the things I heartily disliked about Max — that he could be right so often, and so utterly conventional in his thinking at the same time.

Naturally all the parents of all the club members admired and approved of him. To them he was a model young man. As for the rest of us — we were just trash. But what they could not deny was that we knew how to enjoy ourselves. They loved to hear us sing and play. As musicians, none of us became anything, by the way. We weren't anything of any account, any of us. These were the few bright years allotted us. After the club broke up we just became the usual run of the mill — workers, parents, nobodies.

Why am I writing this book, I ask myself. Most of the events narrated I have dwelt on at length in other books of mine. Yet I feel compelled to relate everything over again, even for the twentieth time. Is it that I am bedazzled by my own life? Do I think my life was so very different from that of most men? I'm afraid I do. And the strange thing is that now, in writing about it again, I can see myself as a person objectively. I am not blind to my own faults or vain about my accomplishments. What I see more and more is the miraculous element in my life. It was a "charmed" life, as they say. I wriggled out of situations which would have killed or ruined other men. I think immediately of one little example.

During the time I was giving piano lessons—for thirty-five cents an hour!—I met, as I said before, the widow at the home of her friend Louise. I was teaching Louise's daughter. After the lessons her mother would send the girl to her room, then try to seduce me. One night I came dangerously close to letting myself be seduced. I didn't know that she had syphilis or that she was being kept by a Negro, the bicycle repair man who took care of me when my bike needed fixing. Ed was his name. Anyway, one night I am standing by the door, saying goodnight to Louise, when we hear a key being put in the lock. Before Ed could open the door she had pushed me behind the curtain. I heard her say, with a quiver in her voice, "Oh Ed, is that you? I didn't expect you so early." He touched me in brushing by me, never suspecting that it was me or anyone else, of course. Had he known I think he would have killed me. I shall always remember how caressingly she said, "Oh Ed, it that *you?*"

"Meet me Tonight in Dreamland" and "Shine on, Harvest Moon, for me and My Gal."

Today they refer nostalgically to the '50s and '60s. When these two songs were the rage—and they were indeed the rage, like no hits we know of today—you might say the world, *our* world was in flower. No one who ever sang these songs has ever forgotten them, I am sure. It was the time of the open trolley car, of Trixie Friganza and Elsie Janis, of George M. Cohan and Charles Chaplin, of the great dance halls, the marathon and little bun-

[99]

ches of violets for your sweetheart. Then New York did seem to have a glamorous side. There were so many celebrities dear to the public's heart. There were great wrestlers, like Jim Londos, for example, or Earl Caddock, the man of a thousand holds, not phonies like today. There were great fighters, like Fitzsimmons, Corbett, Jim Jeffries, Jack Johnson. There were the six-day bike riders and polo players. Football and basketball were virtually out of the picture. An Elvis Presley was unthinkable, as was a crazy loon like Moon Dog Main, who eats glass and swallows live gold fish.

I can still see myself at the piano, pulling out of my music roll a song Cora would like. My favorite, of course, was "Meet me Tonight in Dreamland." That's where I spent most of my time — in Dreamland. Strange that I never thought of fucking her. Not that she was too sacred, too holy to be fucked. No, it was Love I felt for Cora, love with a capital L that reached to the skies. And I never mixed the two — love and sex, which shows what an imbeile I must have been.

How wonderful to be sitting beside her in the open trolley, on our way to Rockaway or Sheepshead Bay, and singing at the top of our lungs — "Shine on, Harvest Moon, for me and My Gal." Or, "I don't want to set the world on fire. . ." How many ditties there were like that in those days! All from Tin Pan Alley, from "little ole Broadway," as we used to say. And what a shit-hole it is today! The glamour has been converted to smut, the celebrities have disappeared, a cunt like Linda Lovelace, who is able to swallow the biggest cock imaginable, is a big name. Just for her ability to do that! Imagine it!

That's why, perhaps, at twenty-one, Max Winthrop and I could play like little boys on that farm in New Jersey where he was convalescing. It was early Spring and the nights and early mornings were bitter cold. We slept under eiderdown quilts, as there was no heat whatever in the bedrooms. Maury, Max's nephew, who was mentally retarded or a bit nuts, perhaps both,

[100]

slept in the same room with us. We would lie awake for hours telling stories or exchanging jokes. Maury looked upon his Uncle Max as Jesus Christ himself. He would have done anything for him. Max, on the other hand, treated his nephew like the imbecile he was, cuffed him, called him names, made him do all manner of things his parents would have disapproved of. The worse he treated the boy, the more the boy revered him. He even, out of gratitude seemingly, dug up some nice young fresh cunt for Max. Served them to him on a silver platter, with a sprig of parsley to give it additional savour. All this horseplay was right up Max's alley. As I said before, he knew how to keep a straight face. Evenings, he would sit at the organ and play hymns for Maury's parents. They hadn't the least suspicion what a jolly monster they were harboring in Max.

In bed Max would keep Maury in stitches, imitating the pious look of his parents. Max could even make them look thoroughly imbecilic without danger of hurting Maury's feelings. Maury laughed easily, laughed at anything Max said. I had to laugh myself. I laughed, knowing well just who and what Max was. At home a good husband, good father, in his office, a good doctor. In the poolroom a shark. On the dance floor a satyr. With his pants down, Priapus himself. And all these characters were combined in the one person known to the world as Max Winthrop, Henry Miller's friend. It was assumed by most everyone that we were such great friends that nothing could ever separate us. No matter how gregarious I was, I was also a loner, very much of a loner. In everything but sociability and camaraderie, I was exceedingly different from the other club members. It was the same thing in the street; everyone considered me to be his friend, his special friend, whereas I was highly indifferent to the fate of my friends. Now and then, to be sure, I did a dramatic thing for one of these friends, such as selling my bicycle or pawning my watch to prevent a friend from going to jail for some petty theft.

One has to be truly adolescent, I suppose, to attach the importance we did to our secret hand-shake, our pass-words, and so

[101]

on. Or to be so genuinely moved at meeting one another again after the lapse of only a week or two. Myself, I was probably the most emotional of all. When I saw Georgie Alford take his violin out of the case and tune up, I was almost in tears. I adored the way he played the instrument. He loved everything in a minor key and was marvelous as a second fiddle. He was also killing himself, with women, liquor and tobacco. He had the consumptive look of a Chopin and when he played it was always with a whole heart. At the same time he was an absolute good-for-nothing — not a redeeming quality in him except for his lovable nature.

In the early days of the Xerxes Society, I was holding a miserable job in a famous cement company. I was a file clerk and evidently not very capable, though an idiot could have filled the job capably. I was too wrapped up in my bicycle, staying up too late with the widow, and of course thoroughly disinterested in my job. The boss who was over me, an irascible Canadian, would fly into a rage over the mistakes I made. I am sure he thought I was mentally deficient. The salary I received was ridiculous. In those days grown men, married, perhaps with children, were paid as little as fifty dollars a month. I think my salary was fifteen or twenty dollars a month.

The only one of us who ever had any money in his pocket was Max Winthrop. He was careful with his money, and thrifty. The rest of us had no sense of the value of money whatever. My lunch money for the week, for example, I could piss away in one night. So the rest of the week I starved or I would borrow a nickel from a fellow worker to buy a chocolate candy bar. I had a sweet tooth. The thirty-five cents I earned for a piano lesson was gone before I got home. I would buy myself two banana splits, which cost me thirty cents. Sometimes I was so disgusted with myself, with the lack of cash, that I would throw the remaining nickel in the gutter. Later, I would be bending over in the rain, to pick up the pennies someone had thrown me out of pity.

I could never imagine Max doing such things. But then I could never imagine him writing a *Tropic of Cancer* or even a Mickey Spillane thriller. One could see his life well in advance — it was as if someone had tattooed a blueprint of it over his body. No surprises, unless for the ability he showed to dig up fresh cunt. I could never imagine him showing a girl much affection — or writing her a love letter. With Max it had to be quick work or nothing. The funny part of it is that Max did not give the impression of a guy who was always on the prowl. The girl herself wouldn't know sometimes that he had his eye on her until she felt his prick inside her. Max would devour her like a sandwich. Then a friendly pat on the rump and ta-ta! That was it. Bye bye, baby! Usually these fucks didn't cost him a penny either. Max's philosophy was simple — if they like you, you can fuck them; if they don't, money won't get you anywhere. In the main he was right. But what sort of trollops were these conquests of his? Some he liked because they had big teats, some because of a cute ass, whatever that might mean, and others because they not only know how to fuck, but because they *loved* to fuck. Those were number-one gals for Max. He never spoke of a girl's beauty. He spoke of separate parts of the body. He could go into dithyrambs for example, about the hair on a certain girl's cunt. Once he raved about a fifteen-year-old who he said loved to do it standing up. In addition she never stopped coming once she started. He was afraid to let her suck him off for fear she would bite his prick off in sheer ecstasy.

There was another member of the club who was as much of a wolf as Max. But I will devote a chapter to him shortly. Anyway, never again have I met two men who were so hungry for cunt, who made it their business, you might say. Neither of them ever spoke of being in love. It was just cunt they were after, or, as they put it, "another piece of tail."

In a way, then, it was as easy "to get one's nookie" in those days as it is today. Men haven't changed much, nor women either. The big difference between those times and this era is that now love is dying out. The songs may be full of love but not men's

[103]

hearts. To be madly in love with someone is to be old-fashioned. Supposedly. That's not true either. The big difference between now and yesterday is that today you don't have to ask anyone's permission. All that matters is that she likes it and wants it. No danger of her becoming an old maid if she has the necessary. Even marriage is no longer important. In my time even if it was only a prostitute you were taking to a hotel room you had to have a suitcase with you and you had to sign the register Mr. and Mrs So and So.

Today a good whore — a call girl let's say — can make a couple of hundred dollars a day and not break her back. In my day you could buy a piece of ass for fifty cents sometimes. Today these gals ride around in cars, have cute apartments of their own, are not diseased and are not out to make a quick buck. You needn't be ashamed to take them to dinner or play a round of golf with them. Some of them are so sportive, and so well read, it's hard to make them keep their mind on the business at hand. They'd just as lief talk about Hemingway or Tolstoy or give you the low-down on Muhammed Ali and Joe Frazier. They're not whores any more. They're bright, educated young women who make a good, clean living at fucking — and they only fuck those they like — what they call "gentlemen."

Today a girl who is eighteen and who hasn't been fucked yet is looked upon as lacking something. Most kids begin at twelve or fourteen. By twenty-one a girl today could have had a hundred different men. Not that that makes her any happier than her counterpart of fifty years ago. Nor does one have to have a great pair of teats today or a cute ass. Just being ready at any time is the essential. One should be able to count up to one hundred, of course. No need to know calculus or higher mathematics. No need to know Shakespeare, Homer or Dante.

Think of the movie stars who came up from the gutter. Who cares? Can she still turn you on, that's all that matters. There was one woman, an entertainer, who had only to sing one song a night to have the whole country at her feet. She didn't have to

[104]

show her belly button or wiggle her ass, or let her teats fall out like a "For Sale" sign; she simply had to sing in her own inimitable way, the song she had made so popular — "Red Head." Irene Franklin was her name. Not a great star, nor a great personality either, for that matter. But she had found what people wanted — a catchy tune. And because of it she could have anything she wanted. There were a number of men and women like that in the old days. Everybody loved them. Who does not remember Jack Norworth and Nora Bayes? They didn't have to be great actors or actresses, they didn't have to be too intelligent either. Nor was their sex life common knowledge. None of them were anything like a Garbo or a Duse. America simply took them to their hearts. Lucky creatures. A type that is growing rarer and rarer. Today it is more apt to be a football star than a stage or movie personality. What I am trying to say perhaps is that there was a light touch to things in the old days, more affection, more warmth, more devotion and loyalty. Advertising was only in its infancy. The public relations man was unknown. Champagne was more in vogue than cocaine.

In the beginning of my life there were books — plenty of them. Everyone who knew me wanted to contribute to my thirst for books. Today I am swamped with books — in many languages. Many I throw in the trash can. I have no respect for books per se. I am almost being buried alive under the avalanche of reading matter. And the more I read the more I realize that there were only a few great ones. I wanted to be one of those, one who would be remembered. And here again was a disturbing difference between Max and myself. He had a reverence for books and little ability, if any, to distinguish between a great author and a mediocre one. He was always baffled by the diversity of authors I pretended to read and admire. For I did not read *all* the books I could talk about so eloquently. Some authors make me drunk before ever reading them. Some were like gods to me, though I never read a line of theirs. I could *sniff* a good book or good author like a dog sniffs a good piece of tail. I didn't have to be in

[105]

rut to tell the difference between a genius and a mere scribbler. I always despised the books we were given to read in school. Max, on the other hand, thought these books were "real literature."

Most people are born blind, deaf and mute. They think that acquiring what is called "Culture" will restore these missing faculties. They learn to recite names — of authors, composers, actors, and so on. They pass these off for the real thing. Lectures, for example, are most important to them: the easy way to imbibe culture. I have always been leery of Culture. Born imitator that he was, Max oozed Culture. If, as he once said, "the sun rose and set in his mother's ass," then Culture might be said to have done the same in *his* ass. Strange, how the ass was such an all important part of the body to him. To hear him rave about so and so's beautiful ass was like listening to Vergil reading from his own "Aeneid."

Like his father — who resembled a French peasant — Max was big, heavy and without subtlety. One would think his thick fingers unwieldy for the piano, but not so. They knew how to "tickle the ivories," as we say. They also knew how to get to the mouth of the womb without wasting time. He could play the "Maple Leaf Rag" like a drunken coon.

As our little differences grew more pronounced, our eventual estrangement became more inevitable. And yet it was not the accumulation of these differences which finally brought about the rupture but something altogether unexpected.

As I have said, it was through Max that I kept track of Cora's doings. His wife knew someone who was very intimate with Cora. Thus I learned that she was planning to become a schoolteacher, something which truly saddened me. Through the same source I learned that she was getting thinner, paler, more serious, which was also depressing news. In short, I counted on Max to keep me posted as to Cora's doings. Sometimes I would inquire timidly if Cora ever asked about me. Evidently she didn't.

However, from another source I learned that she did inquire about me from time to time. By a curious coincidence, her brother-in-law, who was rather wealthy, was one of my father's customers. He knew about Cora and me and would volunteer information about her whenever he visited my father's shop. Usually he would tease me for not being more aggressive. He would warn me to wake up or she might fall in love with someone else. (Strangely enough, I never gave this possibility much thought. I always saw Cora as being there, waiting for me—until eternity.) Yet we never telephoned one another, nor did we exchange more than three or four letters a year. Her letters were thoroughly conventional—her handwriting inflamed me more than her words. We just were not made to be together in this life. In some other time—past or future, maybe, but not this one. To think of her in bed with another man, a husband perhaps, was impossible for me. She did not belong to that race of women who took out a license and then permitted themselves to be raped night after night. And yet. . .

We are coming to it. In one night all my illusions are shattered. In one night all my hopes are dashed, all my feelings smashed. A pure accident. We are on that farm in New Jersey. It is night time and we are telling one another stories while snuggling under the cosy eiderdown.

Suddenly, out of the blue, I ask Max if he's heard anything about Cora lately. I hadn't any news about her for over a year.

"I think she's O.K.," Max replied.

"You *think*," I repeated. "Don't you *know*? Doesn't your wife see their mutual friend any more?"

"Sure, Myrtle still sees her, only now that Cora's married—"

I sat bolt upright in bed. *"Married,"* I roared. *"Since when!* You never told me she was married."

"I did too, Hen, only you weren't paying attention, I guess."

"When was this?" I asked.

"Oh, a year or so ago. You had just left home to live with the widow."

I shook my head in disbelief. Cora married—impossible.

"What sort of guy did she marry?" I asked.

[107]

"A nice guy," says Max. "A chemist or a physicist, I think."

"How long had they been going together?"

"Oh, a year or so. . . You see, Hen, when Cora found out about the widow that finished it."

"How did she find out?"

"Ask me. News travels, you know. Besides, she ran into you two at the beach once, remember? That was quite a blow to her. Then, when she heard you were living together, well you can put two and two together."

I was only half-listening to his words. I was furious, furious at him, for not telling me sooner, and more furious because he was taking it so matter of factly.

"You know what I ought to do to you?" I yelled. "I ought to beat the living shit out of you."

This time *he* sat straight up in bed. Maury urged us to moderate our voices or we would wake the old folks.

"Listen, Hen," Max begins. "You've been acting strangely ever since you took up with the widow. You're jumpy, edgy—you're not yourself any more. We've all urged you to give her up but you turn a deaf ear. You don't see—" He broke off abruptly.

"Don't see what?" I asked.

"You don't see how incongruous it looks to see you going with a woman old enough to be your mother."

"No, I don't," I replied. "She doesn't look old. Besides, thirty-seven or eight isn't old."

"No," said Max, "It's just the difference between you. It ain't natural."

"But I—" I cut it short, I was just about to say—"But I love her." In my strange was I suppose I did love her, though I told myself it was pity which kept me tied to her. That was a lie, of course. A man doesn't fuck a woman night after night, in bed, on a chair, under the table—out of pity. The truth of the matter was every day I was thinking how to disengage myself. She knew I loved Cora, though we seldom spoke of her. Now, as I found out the next day, the house Cora and her husband lived in was on the

[108]

next street to ours. Her house, in fact, was directly opposite ours. We both occupied top floors. With a spyglass I could look through my back window directly into hers — into her bedroom no less, that room which I didn't want to know existed. And this had been going on for over a year. Somehow I couldn't bring myself to believe it. And I hated, despised and loathed Max for telling me. I had rather he lied to me. I could not and never would, never did, forgive him.

Facing East — Henry Miller 1942

Red brick house on the right—
622 Driggs Avenue, where I
lived until I was nine.

CHAPTER SEVEN

Alec Considine

I'm not sure if it was from Galway
or County Cork that his parents hailed but they were as Irish as
Paddy's pig. His old man was a hod carrier and looked the part.
His mother was more like a blue-nosed Nova Scotian than an
Irish biddy. The old man threw tantrums now and then. He was
crabby and cantankerous. He could get hopping mad and actually dance with rage. If I thought my home life was difficult
Alec's was a hundred times worse. His old man was a constant
source of humiliation to him. The old man was that ignorant he
had never heard of Robert Burns. Add to this that he was a
prejudiced, narrow-minded Catholic, stubborn and obstinate as
they make 'em.

Alec was from the old neighborhood though not attending the
same school as I. He was going to a business school, learning
stenography and typewriting. He intended to become a public
stenographer while putting himself through college.

[111]

It was through Max Winthrop that I met Alec. They lived in the same neighborhood. The fact that Alec's father and mother came from Ireland meant they might just as well have come from another planet. Alec's ways were incomprehensible to them and theirs to him. There was no possibility of understanding one another.

Like my friend Jimmy Pasta, he too nourished ambitions though he had not definitely made up his mind what he intended to be. First of all he wanted a good education.

It was with Alec that I had the greatest rapport, as far as intellectual matters were concerned. Whereas Max Winthrop was thoroughly conventional in his thinking—if not in his behavior—Alec Considine was a rebel and a radical right down to the bone. We were always arguing and discussing things, chiefly about books and world events. Many a night it was four or five in the morning before we would separate.

If we happened to see a good play, say by Shaw, Galsworthy or O'Neill, we could mull over it for weeks. Of course we had both read the great European dramatists, such as Ibsen, Ernst Toller, Strindberg, the German Expressionists and so on. We were both voracious readers and we rather looked down upon the other members of the Club for their ignorance.

The chief obsession of his was—as with Max Winthrop—*cunt*. It didn't matter what she looked like, how ignorant she might be—was she fuckable? That was all he was interested in. Every so often he got the clap which didn't bother him too much: he treated it like a cold in the head. Also, it seemed to make him even hornier.

What he liked was to find a good-natured whore, fuck her in her own room, then bolt without paying her.

Of course he liked the dance halls. Not the ones with taxi girls but the dives where girls went to pick up men and vice versa. He drank heavily, but that was a natural part of his Irish background. His old man hailed from the slums. It was amusing how well I got along with his parents. They thought me to be

quite a gentleman; they liked the respectful way in which I addressed them and my behavior in general. Why couldn't their
Alec be like me? In their eyes he was nothing more than a bum,
he would never be anybody or get anywhere. (I should add that
my own parents thought pretty much the same about me. They
were particularly critical of my association with Alec.)

However, he fooled them all. He made his way through
business school, then college with a Master's degree. What now?
he asked himself. What was he going to do for a living? All this
did not improve him. He was incorrigible.

It was through a strange coincidence that he happened to
decide on the career of architect. Someone had lent him a book
about the famous Sullivan of Chicago, forerunner of Frank
Lloyd Wright. That decided him. He would give New York some
buildings to remember. And, strange to say, he did just that
eventually.

But I'm getting ahead of myself.

One of the things that irritated him about me was that I was
always broke. Wherever we went he paid the bill, but not without
a lot of grumbling and cursing. He used to lecture me about my
lack of ambition. What was I going to become eventually? He
knew, to be sure, that I was writing, or trying to write, but this
never impressed him much.

My first wife hated him. She knew what Alec was like and
would always try to hold me back when he asked me to go out
with him. Alec had watched me go through my ordeals with Cora
and the widow and knew I wouldn't last long with the wife. "I
didn't suggest you marry her," he said to me once. "I only said
she would make a good lay."

Incredible as it may seem, I fought with her every day. There
wasn't a single thing we ever agreed about. She had been reared
in a Catholic school, later a Catholic conservatory of music in
Canada, and was naturally filled with all sorts of wrong ideas. In
spite of their rigid moral codes and stupid beliefs some of her
Catholic friends were good sex pots. I remember one who used to

finger her rosary and, while fucking away for dear life, would exclaim, "O mother of God, O blessed Virgin, forgive me for what
I am doing!" And so saying, she would grab my cock and hold it
in her hand a while, caress it, kiss it, then shove it back in her
cunt and whisper—"Do it some more, Henry, it feels so good.
Fuck me, fuck me! And may the holy Virgin forgive and protect
me!"

What Alec liked was nurses. They knew how to protect themselves, they were free in their ideas, and easy to manipulate.
Many was the nurse he fucked in the park, her back up against a
tree. Like another bosom pal of ours, he didn't believe in
spending money unnecessarily on women. On the other hand, he
would tell them he loved them. He would say anything, even
promise to marry, so long as he could get his end in.

The exciting thing was our conversations and discussions.
Being Irish he had a flair for argument and dispute. But he was a
logician too. Anything and everything was food for argument.
He also enjoyed giving advice but was seldom able to take any
himself. Our best talks occurred in his room. Unlike my hall
bedroom, which was more like a prisoner's cell, his room was
spacious, boasted a sink with running water, a couch, a couple of
comfortable old chairs and a huge bed. He got up when he damn
well pleased. Sometimes there was a girl in bed with him. He
would introduce her in a casual way, pretending to know her a
long time. "This is the kid I've been telling you about, Hen," he
would say, pulling the covers off her to expose her charms. Patting her belly or her rump he would add—"Not bad, eh?"

One of the things about our relationship was the intimacy we
indulged in. We were more like two Russians out of Dostoievsky
than natives of Brooklyn.

If he had the clap, for instance, he would get out of bed, ask
me to approach the sink, then take out his cock—a dreadful
sight—and ask me in all seriousness if I thought he should see a
doctor about it. While holding it in his hand—it looked like a
bloody sausage—he would begin a long story about some girl he

[114]

had met and her relations with the parish priest. (He hated the Catholic church like poison.) "Listen, Hen, get this," he would begin. "She goes to confession and this time she has to confess that she has just had her first experience with a man."

Here's how the dialogue went. . . He imitates the pious, honey-tongued hypocrite, Father O'Reilly.

Father: "You say you let him touch you. Just *where* did he touch you, my child?"

The girl is too embarrassed to reply immediately. The Father tries to help her out.

Father: "Did he touch your breast, my child?"

"Yes, Father."

Father: "Tell me, where else did he put his hand?"

"Between my legs," she replies.

"Did he leave it there long? I mean — ten minutes, twenty-five minutes or an hour?"

"Nearer to an hour, I guess, Father."

"And what did *you* do all that time?"

"I got very excited, Father. I lost my head completely, I fear."

"What do you mean by that, child?"

(Mind you, this "child" is about eighteen, built like a race horse.)

"I mean, Father, that then he unbuttoned his trousers, took out his thing and put it where he had his hand before."

"Did he put it inside you?"

"Yes, Father, he did."

"Did it feel good or were you very ashamed of yourself?"

"It felt terribly good, Father. I'm afraid I may let him do it again — that is, if it isn't too great a sin."

"We'll see about that later," says Father O'Reilly. "Now I want you to step into my office for a few minutes."

"You can imagine the rest, Hen. He gets her into his office, asks her to lift her dress so that he can fiddle with her vagina, and then, in the twinkling of an eye, he's got his prick out and fucking the B'Jesus out of her.

[115]

"That's an everyday occurrence. That's nothing compared to what took place a few centuries ago. The Popes, some of them, were not only thieves and murders, they committed incest too." He went to his bookcase and pulled out a book on the lives of the Popes. "Here, read this sometime when you have nothing better to do."

Then, with a strange smile on his face, he quickly adds —"What do you do with yourself all day, may I ask? Don't tell me you're sitting in the library reading all day. I suppose you're still looking for a job. By the way, how much dough have you on you now? Can you return that dollar I lent you last week?"

I made a wry grimace and pretended to laugh it off.

I pulled my empty pockets out to show him I was telling the truth.

"I can't get over it," he says. "Always stone broke. Tell me, Hen, how do you manage to get around? Do you scrounge from everyone you meet? Don't you have any pride? I won't speak of ambition. I know that would be inconsistent with your philosophy." This was intended sarcastically, because I was always telling him of the philosophers I was reading.

"I suppose," he went on, "your Prince Kropotkin never used money. And what about that German philosopher who ended up in the nut house?"

"You mean Nietzsche?" I said.

"Yeah, that's the guy. Didn't he think he was another Jesus?"

I pretended to be surprised.

"On the contrary," I said, "you forget that it was he who wrote *The Anti-Christ*."

A pause, during which he applies some ointment to his sore, swollen prick, then sinks slowly, like a Pasha, back into the bed. From the bed—

"O, Hen, before I forget—open the top drawer of that dresser. In a tray you'll find some change. Help yourself! That'll save you the trouble of asking me later." An afterthought — "By the way, if I hadn't offered you a little money how would you have got home — tell me that, will you?"

I had to smile. "O, I always manage somehow," I said.

"*You* manage?" he repeated. "You mean someone always manages to rescue you at the last minute."

"Righto," I said. "It comes to the same thing, doesn't it?"

"It does to you, maybe, but not to me."

"Why do you worry yourself about these things?" I asked.

"Because I haven't anything better to do, I guess. Listen, Hen, don't take me seriously. I'm just as much of a bum as you, only I'm a little smarter. I like to poke my nose into everybody's business. By the way, would you write down the titles of those books you were talking about yesterday?"

"What's the use?" I replied. "You'll never read them. They're not the kind of books that get you anywhere."

"You don't have to tell me that," he said. "Sometimes I wonder what *you* see in them. That Dostoievsky of yours, for instance. Just the other day I picked up one of his novels, thinking to read it. But Jesus, he takes up twenty or thirty pages describing how someone bends over to pick up a tooth pick. He may be great for the Russians — not for me. I know you dote on him. But then you have nothing better to do. Anyway, Hen, put the titles down for me, will you? Who knows, I *may* read them before I die."

I jotted down a few titles with the names of the authors.

"How do you come by such books?" he says. "Now this one, about Milarepa — is that how you pronounce it? What has he got to give *me*?"

"Why don't you read and find out for yourself?" I suggested.

"Because I'm too damned lazy, I guess," he answers bluntly.

As I'm getting ready to leave he suddenly remembers something.

"Listen, Hen, I almost forgot. You know what? I think I'm falling in love. In fact, I may be in love already. It's someone I never spoke to you about. Someone who won't let me touch her. A school teacher *and* a Catholic. Can you beat that? Yeah, every time I call on her I bring a box of candy or flowers. She thinks

[117]

that's refined. In her eyes I'm pretty low in the scale. She says I'm intelligent but I have no principles. She's trying to make a gentleman of me, can you beat that? That's why I've got to get this dose of clap cured soon. I don't know what she'd say or do if she saw what it looks like now. That's why I asked you about the books. I can rattle off the titles—that will impress her. She says she reads a lot, but I don't think it's great literature. She likes to go to the opera and the ballet. The movies are too vulgar for her. Doesn't know much about art. I don't think she'd know a Gauguin from a Van Gogh. She'd like me to take piano lessons. I told her about you. She seemed impressed. Of course I didn't tell her what an unreliable irresponsible bastard you are."

I tried to find out her name but he wouldn't give it to me. "You won't like her, I think," he says. "Too damned refined, too conventional. She'd like your intellect though. And your smooth talk. By the way, how is it going with the widow? Still in love with her? Look out or she'll have you marrying her before long."

"She's already tried," I said. And I related how I had told my mother one day while sitting in the kitchen—told her I was going to marry the widow. I had hardly got the words out of my mouth when my mother approaches me with a carving knife in her hand. "Another word of this," she exclaimed, "and I'll plunge this through your heart." By the look on her face I believe she would have.

"Your folks are almost as bad as mine," says Alec. "You should hear my old lady sometime. She sounds cracked to me, B'Jesus. And the old man is worse. Such moralistic monsters—from the Emerald Isle, no less."

At this juncture I thought it appropriate for him to let me dig into his coffer again.

"How much did you take the first time?" he wanted to know.

"About sixty cents," I told him.

"O.K. Take another thirty-five cents, if you like, but no more. I have to work for my money," he added.

I agreed, but just the same I took fifty cents. I didn't mind

[118]

cheating and robbing him. It made up for all the sermons he delivered. In a good mood he might lend me as much as five dollars, but it was like pulling teeth. Some days he had fifty or a hundred dollars on him. He bet on the horses frequently and won.

As I'm easing my way out he cries out — "Hen, what was that title of the Dostoievsky novel you mentioned the other day? I want to tell my girl."

"*The Idiot*," I yelled back.

"Thanks, Hen, I'll try her out with that one first. What a title! Is it really about an idiot?"

"Yes, Alec, but a most exceptional one. He'll put your girl in a trance."

It was always hard to take leave of him or to get rid of him if he came to see me. Soetimes, if I were reading an interesting book, for example, I would not answer a knock at the door. If it were Alec I would know it quickly, for he hated to be left standing in the hallway.

"It's me, Hen, it's Alec!" he would shout, rapping harder.

Then I would grow quiet as a mouse, hardly daring to breathe. After a time he would give up and descend the stairs. But sometimes he would try to fool me. (He always knew that I was in.) He would descend the steps noiselessly, in the expectation that I would believe he had gone and might open the door just to see. Sometimes we would carry on this game for an hour or more. It was always something urgent he had to see me about. At least, it seemed so to him. To me nothing was urgent, nothing important, particularly if I were reading a good book. In those days I could read for hours at a stretch. Later on, when I began writing in earnest, I wouldn't dream of wasting my time reading in broad daylight. I almost regarded reading as sinful. Strange change of outlook. But in becoming a writer I had undergone many changes of viewpoint. In any case, reading had now become a luxury with me. I permitted myself this luxury with only a few special writers, to wit — Dostoievsky, Oswald Spengler,

[119]

Elie Faure, Sherwood Anderson, Rimbaud, Giono, and such like. I never read a popular novel. Neither did I read the newspaper in those days. I was thoroughly disinterested in the news. If there were war or revolution, I always said, I would soon hear about it. The rest meant nothing to me. There was no television then, nor radio either. I disliked the radio when it did come. The radio was for half-wits and simpletons, I told myself. Or housewives who had nothing better to do.

And so I read a great deal. My friend Alec absorbed my reading like a sponge. He always referred to my favorite writers as "queer birds" not meaning "homosexual" to be sure, but eccentric, slightly cracked, or downright mad. For a writer to be mad was o.k. in his opinion. An artist had to be a bit mad to survive in a world such as ours. Such opinions led him to say to me, when in the mood, "You know, Hen, I think you have it in you. At any rate, you're crazy enough to pass for an artist. *All you lack is talent*." I don't recall ever showing him anything I had written which he approved. "In the first place," he would say, "you use too many big words, you know that." Indeed I did. I knew that he was slowly reading the entire unabridged dictionary, which then contained about a half a million words. And how did he read this huge tome? By tearing out a fresh page every day and sticking it in his coat pocket. In the subway, on a bus, or while waiting to see someone in his office, he would pull out the page and study it. He took notice not only of the definition of the words, but of their pronunciation and derivation. So at times he would correct my usage of a word or its pronunciation.

Apotheosis was such a word. I pronounced it a*poth*eosis. The correct way was apoth*e*osis. He loved to trip me up occasionally. Sometimes he would call me up at some ungodly hour to ask if I knew such and such a word.

But it was not only that I used big words which bothered him — it was that my stories were dry and dull. I ought to read de Maupassant, he averred, or Somerset Maugham. They knew their craft! He was right, they were indeed good craftsmen, but

[120]

then I didn't attach much importance to "craft." My favorites had gone far beyond mere craft. They were writing from their guts or perhaps some stranger part of the body. They didn't care about being understood by any and everybody. They addressed themselves to the elite, to their peers. Oddly enough, in doing so, they not only reached their peers but oddballs like me or simpletons who didn't read much. Actually, of course, they were writing to please themselves. They did not have to meet any requirements. They had no boss and no steady income. Most of them were recognized fifty years too late.

Alec couldn't understand anyone putting up with such delays. He wanted to see results — and quickly. A genius like Van Gogh, who never sold even one painting during his entire life was not only a genius, in Alec's opinion, but a fool. He could have painted signs or houses, in Alec's mind, instead of sponging on his brother.

Nevertheless, he was intensely curious about such men. He raved about Maugham's book on Gauguin — *The Moon and Six Pence*. He even liked the idea that Gauguin had left a cushy job in a bank and a good-looking wife, in order to go to Tahiti and paint.

"That's what may happen to you one day," he said. "I can just see you picking up your rags and going to the Himalayas." What I found fascinating about Asia and Asiatics was hard for him to understand.

I pointed out that our own Lafcadio Hearn of New Orleans, whose stories he professed to like, had left America to go to Japan, where he married a Japanese woman and wrote most of his work. "Yes, Hen," he said, "but remember that Hearn himself was a cross between a Greek and an Irishman. He wasn't a typical one hundred percent American."

I didn't see that that mattered. I talked about Marco Polo and similar adventurers. He was unimpressed.

"You dote on crackpots and eccentrics," he said.

For all the criticism that he heaped on me, he had a strong

[121]

affection for me. I think he secretly regretted being so "normal" and "conventional" himself. Though few people who knew him would have used those adjectives in referring to him.

Certainly there was nothing unusual in the way he dressed. Unless it was that he was unusually sloppy and dirty. (He used to pin notes on the mirror at the sink, reminding himself to wash his *whole body,* not just his hands and face.) Now and then he would ask me to come close and sniff him. "Tell me honestly," he would say, "do I smell bad? I'm so damned lazy I hate to bother to wipe my ass. That's the truth."

To tell the truth, he sometimes did smell bad. He always had a bad breath, for one thing. That was because of his drinking and smoking and his neglect in brushing his teeth. "Look at them," he would sometimes remark, "aren't they disgusting? They look more like fangs than teeth, don't they?" As you can see, he was not in the least ashamed of admitting his weaknesses and defects. In fact, he took pleasure in airing them — at least with me. His idea of a friend was one to whom you could tell anything about yourself. If it were incest, all the merrier.

He could smell like a horse *and* stable! Often he got into bed with his shoes on. Or he would get out of bed and shine his shoes with the bed sheet. Living like a pig and behaving like a bum, it sounded strange, coming from him, to advise his sister how to behave with men. She was not to trust *any* of them — good advice! — not even the well-behaved ones. And especially the smooth talkers. (Well he might warn her of that type, for he was one of the smoothest talkers imaginable.)

The truth is, I guess, that we were both the confessor type. Yet to this day I have not read Jean Jacques Rousseau's *Confessions*. I have read most of the great confessions, such as the one by Saint Augustine. And the one by the celebrated young woman — Marie Bashkirtseff — and the *Diary of Amiel (Le Journal Intime)*. The one great confession (in thirteen volumes) which everyone seems to have read, I gave up half-way through the first volume. I am referring to the great Don Juan — Casanova — to his *Memoirs*.

These were the sort of books Alec loved to hear me talk about but, as he said, never had time to read.

He did find time, of course, to read *Fanny Hill's Diary.* But what a shrinking violet of a book compared to *My Secret Life*, written by an anonymous gentleman of the Victorian era. I believe I communicated to him my passion for the works of Knut Hamsun, and to my surprise, he read two or three of his books, admitting for once, that my taste was good. But then, seldom in my life have I met anyone who did not share my love for Hamsun. Somewhere in his work Joseph Delteil writes that anyone who does not love his mother is a monster. I would say the same, only substituting for mother Knut Hamsun. There were a few good authors Alec adored aside from those I recommended. Oddly enough, two of them were Stasiu's favorites—Joseph Conrad and Anatole France. He also admired Jack London and Maxim Gorky, the Russian. They had much in common, to be sure. Both men were translated in over fifty languages, including Chinese and Japanese. Both men were trained in "The University of Life," which is the title of a film devoted to Gorky's life. I believe that both men were voracious readers, though neither had much schooling. Both men appealed to a wide audience; both were men of heart and wrote from the heart as well as the guts. With such men it matters little what language they choose to write in—they are understood everywhere by everybody.

There was nothing one could conceal from Alec. He was nosy, inquisitive and a gossiper. He fed on other people's disasters.

Even though he had "almost" fallen in love with his school teacher, he was still on intimate terms with a blonde called Lila and her older sister. It seems that he would go to bed with the two of them. Then, when one of the sisters had fallen asleep, he would quietly put the boots to the other one. As you can imagine, it was a very touchy situation. The more so since it was understood he was going to marry Lila, the younger sister—i.e. when he could afford to marry. He always managed to leave himself a loophole. In one of his frank moods he told me one day

[123]

that he preferred fucking the older sister—not because she was more experienced but because she was more neurotic. Indeed, she was always on the border of hysteria. That heightened the play, he affirmed. But he had to be very careful when fucking this one while her sister was in bed with them. When she got carried away she could squeal like a dog or bite or pinch.

But Alec loved these dangerous situations. If caught he always found a way to wriggle out. He was not only a first rate liar, he was a good actor too. I could very well imagine him in court defending a client. Criminals seemed to fascinate him. Yet Dostoievsky's *Crime and Punishment* left him cold. Sentimental, he called it. He wanted me to know that it wasn't *Crime and Punishment*, but *The* Crime and *The* Punishment. Whereupon, I told him that he was a living example of "the crime" and "the punishment." He was the crime and the punishment all in one. Instead of the prosititute—Sonia, was it?—he had his school teacher friend. He didn't think this at all funny.

If I dwell on his weaknesses it's because, as with Max Winthrop, I am unable to understand how a person can get away with so much right under one's nose.

My parents liked Alec Considine because he was "serious" (sic) and ambitious. They didn't know of or suspect his affairs with women, his doses of the clap, his gambling habits, his general filthiness and so on. But parents are not very good judges of other's children. Nor of their own, for that matter. "Don't give us any trouble," that's always their main concern.

Alec's mother resembled one of those blue nosed Nova Scotians, as I said earlier. For some strange reason in that tiny corner of the world the Lord has turned out some of the most unprepossessing women in the world. Of course Mrs. Considine was Irish, but what matter? She carried with her that icy chill, that too correct deportment, that uncharitable look in the eye. She saw nothing good in anyone, friend or foe. She hated herself—and for no particular reason. She was all malice and venom. And her chief affliction, it goes without saying, was her son. When things became intolerable she would call *my* mother to discuss the situation with her. Fortunately, my mother was always eager to get Mrs. Considine off the hook. She said it was impossible to understand her because of her thick brogue. Besides, my mother was not the "simpatico" type. She had her own troubles, she would say. (And I was one of them.)

Though he pretended, Alec, to look after me, it was really I who was looking after him. The only difference was that I did not relish the job, whereas he did. Every day he had to see me, for one reason or another. If I were home (in the evening) he would telephone and tell me where to meet him. I hated the phone — even then — but that didn't matter to him. One of the funny things he was doing was studying the piano. I say funny because he had no ear, no flair whatever for music. I took him to hear one or two Wagnerian operas, during which he fell asleep. He did not know one composer from another. Brahms he had never heard, nor Schumann, nor Ravel, nor Dubussy. He liked only "light things," he said. It was the same with painting. He had no eyes for painting. Only literature interested him — and the stage. It was about this time that David Belasco was all the rage — and his mistress, whom he had made famous. (Leonore Ulric.) The American theatre was at a low point then — it only began to pick up in the Twenties and Thirties. The Jewish Theatre was much better than the American. With the Theatre Guild came some wonderful plays, such as Tchekov's and Tolstoy's — also Andreyev's and Gorky's. I think it was in this period that I saw "The Dybbuk," performed by the Habima Players. I saw it first in Hebrew, then in Yiddish and finally in English. Unforgettable. Exoricism. But utterly unlike the one now creating such a rage. To close the diversion, like Frank Harris, one of my favorite writers, so one day walked David Belasco into my father's shop. I remember distinctly that he wore his white collar turned backwards, like a priest or minister. I was impressed, naturally. He was one of the very few great personalities I had met thus far.

[125]

To come back to Alec. . . . Yes, he thought he was teaching me — "wising me up" as he put it. In other words, teaching me sophistication. To me it was quite a joke of course. I never liked any of his companions, male or female. I never gambled, I didn't drink. And I was not a good storyteller. In short, I was dull company, which would lead him later, as we rode home, to expand on what a queer fellow I was. Snobbish, he thought. Choosy. Couldn't tolerate "ordinary" people. (To me his "ordinary" people belonged in the zoo.) Unhappy I was, he thought unless I could rave about Nietzche, Dostoievsky, Andre Gide, and such like.

Sometimes, when he wanted to show off in front of a girl, a new one, he would mention the name of some unusual author or the title of one of his books. He would pretend, of course, that he was also familiar with the author. One of these titles he liked to reel off was *Postprandial Conversations*. (Postprandial meaning nothing more than "after dinner.") Of course the girl, impressed by the unfamiliar word, would exclaim — "What is that about, in Heaven's name?" Then Alec would prod me to tell about the book. I usually invented something out of my head — it made no difference since neither of them had read the book. Which reminds me that, though I was not what is called a good storyteller, I could on occasion, especially with unenlightened people, make things up which were far better, far more exciting than mere storytelling. Sometimes I even ventured some psychic tricks, which never failed to stupefy my listeners. Later, Alec would ask quite seriously if there was anything to that yarn I had told at the table. He believed in my ability to read people. Whenever he was in doubt about someone he would invite me to go with him and look them over. He never took my advice, however. Himself, he was full of stories and jokes of all kinds. He usually began the conversation this way — "Listen, Hen, here's one I heard yesterday. You've got to listen to it. . ."

Max Winthrop was equally good at stories and especially at jokes. He had a better sense of humor than did Alec. Sitting in the back room of a saloon, drinking nothing stronger than beer, we could sit up for hours amusing one another. Now and then one of us would piss in his pants from laughing so hard.

As I said, I was getting an education, "getting wised up," as he put it. I learned many things I never put to use and hardly anything that was of any value to me. Except one thing: *people*. All my life I had this faculty of meeting people, of studying them, of being part of them. It matters little from what class they came, what education they had, and so on. Fundamentally all are alike. Yet each one is unique. Strange paradox. All are reachable—and redeemable. Those in prison are often better than those who put them there. Thieves and pimps are far more interesting than preachers and teachers—or most psychologists. Nobody should be wholly despised. Some should be murdered perhaps, in cold blood. But not all murderers are murderers at heart. I have often wondered how many people I have met in my long life. I know for certain that during the four and a half years I spent in the Western Union I met and talked to a good hundred thousand. And yet I regard myself as a loner. I don't mind being alone. As I said somewhere else—"At the worst I am with God!"

That was one thing Alec could not stand. Being alone. It didn't matter whom he chose—he had to have company. I must confess, most of my freedom to be alone developed after I became a writer. Before that I too was always in search of someone. One would think it would be the contrary, that after becoming famous the world would be at one's feet. It happened to me also, but I soon learned how to get rid of these fawns and lickspittles. No, most all the material in my books—people, places, events—happened *before* I began to write. What I enjoy now is to walk in a crowd and be unrecognized. Or perhaps recognized by some very unimportant person—a waitress, a chambermaid, such like. Or, as in France, to be recognized by a butcher or baker, asked to wait a moment till he or she fetches an armful of my books and humbly asks for my autograph. That

[127]

only happens to me in foreign countries. In this country, people in such trades are usually illiterate, or at least *"inculte"* as the French say.

As I have mentioned before, in Alec's eyes I was not yet a writer and probably never would be. Like Stanley, he seemed pleased to think of me as a failure. "I don't know what I find in you that makes me seek you out," he would say to my face. "Maybe it's because you're a good listener."

Anyone who knew us well could see in a minute what drew us together. It was the very difference between us that acted as an attraction. That and the fact that he liked complications. He also adored the same actresses that I did—Elsie Ferguson, Marie Doro, Nazimova, Elsie Janis, Olga Petrova and so on.

From an intense and prolonged discussion of the relative merits of Dostoievsky, Tolstoy, Tchekov, Andreyev, we could move to a poolroom and shoot pool the rest of the night. At midnight I would often go back to his room and discuss, or argue, the merits of other writers. We never tired of talking, arguing, discussing.

We seemed to know every intimate detail of each other's life. We delighted in telling of the weaknesses and foibles of our parents. Which brings me back to Max Winthrop and the backrooms of saloons. Especially that delicious phrase he let drop one night. About his mother—how the sun rose and set in her ass. When he said it Alec and I looked at each other with the same expression of disbelief, of stupor. But we said nothing. We left soon thereafter. It was only a few nights later that Alec brought up the subject.

"I didn't think he was quite that bad," he ventured. "What sentimental rot!"

I agreed—I had never heard worse.

Suddenly I said—"But Alec, maybe she thinks the same of Max, that he's her whole world."

"Then they're both stupid idiots," said Alec. "If they had said it, or felt that way, about Jesus or the Buddha, I could under-

[128]

stand—but about one another! No, that's too much. You know, Hen, sometimes I think Max isn't very intelligent. He knows how to get good marks, pass tests, and that sort of thing, but when it comes to looking at the world he's just a baby. Have you ever noticed?"

One day, in the course of our converstaion, one of those conversations out of a book, he says to me—

"You know, Hen, I'm really not such a bad guy as people like to think. It's true, I'm a bit of a lecher, I drink too much and all that, but I have a good heart. I don't take advantage of people. Now *you*, you bastard, you have a touch of evil in you. I may act like a character in a novel, but it's only acting, whereas you *are* a character in a book—a book that has yet to be written, of course. I *enjoy* making people dislike me. But *you*, you don't seem to care whether you're liked or disliked. You act as if you were a superior being. Where do you get that stuff, I wonder? What gives you such ideas? Probably the books you read. You don't read books the way other people do—you live them! One day you are Glahn the hunter, the next day Alyosya and another day Martin Eden. The only difference between you and these book characters is that you have your eyes wide open. You know what you're doing and where you're going. You can let yourself be inflated by lofty ideas, yet not hesitate to steal a dime from a blind newspaperman.

"You never criticize me or preach to me, but you can make me feel like a worm. Sometimes I wonder why you bother to associate with someone like me. It doesn't seem to matter much to you whom you associate with. All that matters is that they can give you a little change or a fat cigar. I can picture you getting along famously with a murderer, if he was taking good care of you. You seem to think the world owes you a living. You want everything your own way, don't you? The idea of working for a living never appealed to you—not because you're lazy but because you think you're above others. There's something perverse about you. You're not only against society, you're against human nature.

[129]

You're not just an atheist—the very idea of a God seems absurd to you. You don't commit any crimes, but you're a criminal at heart. You talk about brotherly love yet you don't give a shit about your neighbor. As for being a friend, you don't know the meaning of the word. To you a friend is someone who helps you out. If he hasn't got what you need, to hell with him. You're one hundred percent selfish, one hundred percent ego.

"Look at you! You sit there listening to my tirade with a smile on your face. Nothing I say makes the least difference to you. You're not a utopist—you're a solipsist."

"O.K., Alec, so I'm a solipsist. But why all this? I haven't asked you for a cent so far today, have I?"

"No, but you will if I know you. You'd even borrow a pair of dirty socks, if you felt like it."

"I might borrow a clean handkerchief from you but never a pair of dirty socks."

Suddenly, with a wry smile, he says—"You would take a penny if I offered it to you, wouldn't you?"

I replied smilingly that I certainly would.

"How come you don't ask for big sums anymore? You're so modest now—a quarter will do, or even a dime."

"That's because I've learned humility," I said with tongue in cheek.

"You mean a half a loaf is better than none, don't you?"

"You could put it that way too," I said. "By the way, don't you ever steal from your mother's purse?" I added.

"I would if I knew where she kept it," he replied. "Why do you ask? *Do you?*"

I nodded. "Only small amounts," I said, "a dime, a quarter maybe, never a half dollar."

"And she doesn't notice it?"

"I suppose not. Or maybe she just can't believe I would stoop that low."

"She doesn't think you're an angel, ees she?"

"I doubt it. Tell me, what exactly does your mother think of *you?*"

[130]

"I'll make it easy for you, Hen — *the worst!*"

"That's refreshing," I said. "It's good to live without illusions."

"Illusions!" he repeated. "That's exactly the word." He seemed awfully pleased with himself at this moment.

"I suppose you think that *I* live with illusions, don't you?"

"N-no, Hen," he replied soberly. "I don't say that. I say you live in a world of unreality. And very comfortably too. Perhaps that's what irritates me — the fact that you don't suffer any. You have no remorse, no regrets, no sense of guilt. You have no conscience, damn you. You behave like an innocent babe. That's another thing I can't stand — this innocence of yours. Or are you only pretending?"

"I see that I'm not going to get much help from you today," I said. "But then I didn't expect any. I've come to give *you* some money — pay back what I owe you."

He began to laugh uproariously. "And how do you know how much you owe me?" he asked tauntingly. "Because I've kept a record of it here in this little book." I opened the book, scanned the pages and said — "Exactly $52.75 — that's what I owe you."

"And you're going to pay me back — now, today?"

"Of course. Why, would you rather I paid you another day?"

He shook his head. "Don't tell me you *inherited* a sum of money," he began.

"No, Alec, I found it in the street. It was in a wallet. I almost tripped over it. Naturally, I went through the wallet, wondering whom it may have belonged to. Would you believe it, I was almost on the verge of returning it to its owner, but then I came across his business card, with a good address, and I decided to keep the money. I had more need of it than he, I'm sure."

"Are you telling me the truth?" he asked, with a smile on his lips.

"Certainly I am. Why would I invent a story like that? Or did you think perhaps I had stolen it?"

"No, Hen, I didn't think anything. I was just curious. People don't pick up wallets in the street every day, you know."

"Especially not with several hundred dollars in it," I said.

[131]

That set him off for some reason. Now suddenly I was in the category of a thief. I should have made an effort to return it to its owner, or else surrendered it to the police.

"*The police!*" I exclaimed. "You must be out of your mind."

He had to admit that handing it over to the police was far-fetched. Now he was curious as to what I would do with the extra money.

"I'll buy some handsome gift for the widow," I said. "She'll appreciate it."

"Are you giving anything to charity?"

"Not this time," I said. "Maybe when I find another."

"Would you lend me any of it if I asked you?" he inquired.

"Why not? Of course! As much as you wish—you name it."

"Thanks, Hen, I don't want a cent. I was just testing you."

I chatted another few minutes, then took leave of him. He seemed very pleased with himself for some reason.

As I was leaving he said—"You don't need to keep that notebook for my account," he said. "I trust you."

I don't know which of his moods I enjoyed most—probably the cantankerous ones. Somehow, no matter how he berated me, no matter how far-fetched his accusations, I remained untouched. He was a study to me, a most interesting one.

He had yet to be put to the test, of course. He was only a student now, a student full of theories and ideals. I had more confidence in my Italian friend, Jimmy Pasta.

But it was exciting to argue with him. And especially to pull his leg.

He knew me inside out—and yet he didn't know me at all. He didn't *want* to know me, the real me. He wanted to preserve this image of me which he had created for himself. He wanted me to become a failure—to prove some vague point of his own. And he certainly did not, could not, believe that I might become a good writer one day.

One day, just like in a Russian novel, who should suddenly appear on the scene but Alec's older brother who had left home quite a few years ago when Alec was just a kid.

Bob, the brother, had apparently traveled all over the world during his absence. He had spent considerable time in Asia, in India more particularly. He had a lot to relate about the customs of the various peoples and their philosophy of life. To Alec's parents it sounded like so much Greek. But they were proud of their son who seemed indeed to be the very opposite of his younger brother.

At first Alec was impressed. In fact he never knew that he had an elder brother. The parents had said nothing about him, thinking he had become a worthless drifter. As for myself I took to him immediately. I was particularly interested in his spiritual and metaphysical ideas. India had become to him something like his true home. The elder Considines were naturally a bit bewildered by the discussions which now ensued between the two brothers and myself.

It took only a few weeks before Alec and his brother were at loggerheads. Alec simply couldn't swallow all the "spiritual non-sense," as he called it, which his brother dished out.

What I wondered was whatever induced this elder brother to return to the parental home. "Just plain homesick," he explained. Also he feared that he was losing his American heritage.

One of the good results of his brother's homecoming was the surprising change that came over Alec after reading a book of Swami Vivekananda's which his brother lent him. The effect was not only astounding but lasting. Alec changed his way of life overnight. He was now more than ever determined to be a great architect. If I was surprised by this about-face his parents were even more so. They attributed it to the brother's influence, which Alec stoutly denied. He maintained that he was capable of doing his own thinking and needed no help from anyone.

All this reminds me of a quotation which his brother dropped now and then. It was from Gautama the Buddha and ran thus: "I obtained not the least thing from complete, unexcelled

[133]

awakening, and it is for this very reason that it is called complete, unexcelled awakening."

There was another line from the Buddha he was also fond of. It was the Buddha's rejoinder to a question put him by a passing stranger. Asked who he was and what he was, the Buddha replied: "I am a man who is awake."

Alec's brother professed to be puzzled that Alec and I could waste so much time discussing literature rather rather than philosophy or life itself. Names like Strindberg, Bergson, Boccaccio meant nothing to him. Whereas to us these authors were the very breath of life. Perhaps this "literature" which we revelled in was our salvation. It helped us to realize that saint and sinner were alike, that holiness could be found in filth and crime as well as in sacrosanct places and individuals. It made us accept the fact that the idiot or simpleton was not only the rival of the man of genius but often his superior. We were able to live on several planes at once. There was no right and wrong, no ugly and beautiful, no true and false — it was all one.

Sometimes, indeed, we must have seemed foolish to others. Some days we were characters out of Tchekhov or Gorky or Gogol. Other days we were out of Thomas Mann. For a whole year I signed my letters "Hans Castorp," from Mann's *Magic Mountain*. The pity is that we had limited ourselves to literature, that we hardly knew anything about the great painters or the great musicians.

We had great enthusiasm, but little reverence. We knew nothing of discipline. We were like wild animals, feeding on whatever was ready to hand. I consider it a wonderful period of my life. We were libertarians and libertines. We owed allegiance to no one.

One day Alec's brother announced quietly that he was leaving for India in a few days. He showed us a photo of a stunning Indian woman whom he said he was going to marry. He had met her at the Aurobindo Ashram. They were going to live in that new planetary city of Auroville near the Ashram. He was going to work as a carpenter and she as a nurse. Everyone seemed to be relieved at the news, especially Alec.

It was as a result of Bob Considine's arrival that I finally broke with the widow for the first time. Bob had introduced me to a very unusual man, an ex-evangelist, named Benjamin Fay Mills. Mills lectured in Carnegie Hall, Town Hall, and such places, on all manner of subjects. It was through him that I first heard of Freud, for example. Anyway, after being admitted (free) to one of his special classes I discovered that he had a brother in California. I induced Mills to give me a letter of introduction to his brother. My thought was to go West and become a cowboy. It was only a month or so later that I left for the West, with what little savings my mother had put aside for me. I left without saying goodbye to the widow. Halfway to my destination I wrote her that I was on my way to Juneau, Alaska, which of course was a lie. I ended up, as one knows from my books, in Chula Vista, just outside San Diego. I never became a cowboy—I was simply another simple, ignorant ranch hand working in a lemon orchard eight or nine hours a day.

It was while working on this ranch that I went one night to San Diego—ostensibly to visit a whore house—but, happening to notice a poster announcing lectures by Emma Goldman, I went to hear her instead and inadvertently thereby changed the whole course of my life. What a glorious feast it was to attend her lectures! Through her I became acquainted with Nietzsche's works as well as those of other distinguished European writers. It was through reading these writers she lectured about that I gradually decided to become a writer myself.

I remember buying one of Nietzsche's books at the end of one of her lectures. It was *The Anti-Christ*. I had quite a job convincing the man who was selling the books that I was capable of swallowing such strong medicine. I must have looked very immature indeed. Perhaps like a yokel as well, since I was still working on the ranch. At any rate, it was through attending her lectures that I got to know all the famous contemporary

[135]

European dramatists, chief among them being Strindberg.

Was it she, I wonder, who introduced me to Hamsun's work? Strange that I cannot remember how, when and where I came across his work! Certainly the acquaintance with the Russian dramatists I owe to her—and certain German and Austrian ones as well. Even Rabindranath Tagore I owe to her! A few months later, back in New York, I had the good fortune to make the acquaintance of a Swami and through him I got to know the work of Swami Vivekananda, for which I am eternally grateful.

As for the romance with the school teacher, a word or two.

Naturally Alec, could not have an affair with her. For weeks she held him in utter contempt, despite the flowers, the chocolates, theatre tickets and so on which he sent her.

Little by little, however, she began to melt. He no longer had to stand outside the door and bid her good-night. Perhaps she felt sorry for him, perhaps she began to see that he had a better side than he first showed.

In all fairness I must say at this point that in addition to his pesky, crotchety, cantankerous side he could also be a charmer. He could even charm my mother who was hardly susceptible to flattery. Never shall I forget my twenty-first birthday. Naturally all the members of the Club and their girlfriends were present. Even Cora, my beloved, came. I remember having one dance with her throughout the evening. My mother, having made a rather tame bowl of punch for us, was horrified to discover later in the evening that someone had spiked it with whisky and brandy. (This was the work of my friend Alec.) To our utter amazement, he brought with him that evening a stunning looking girl—quite a lady I might say—who was endowed with a remarkable voice. When she opened her mouth to sing "Kiss Me Again," it seemed as if we were listening to our idol Elsie Ferguson.

Toward the end of the evening I noticed that Alec and two or three other fellows had disappeared. Knowing that the punch had had its effect on everyone I thought that they had probably

gone for a bit of fresh air. To my surprise, I heard them dropping a rather heavy load at the top of the stoop. What was it, but
a huge bread box such as grocers used to leave outside their store
at night. As I opened the front door to see what was going on I
noticed that my mother was right behind me. At this moment
Alec and another fellow tipped the bread box on end and sent it
flying down the stoop. My mother uttered an exclamation of
horror and started calling them dirty loafers, all of them. To my
amazement Alec went up to my mother, reached for her lifeless
hand and almost with tears in his eyes said, "Dear Mrs. Miller,
you must forgive us. You see Henry has only one twenty-first
birthday in his whole life and I wanted to make sure that he
would never forget it." My mother started to say something about
the smashed steps of the stoop but he quickly stopped her words
by saying, "Don't worry about the damage to the steps, Mrs.
Miller, *I* will see to it myself that they are repaired. Thank you
very much for the wonderful evening you have given us." And
with that he took off.

Vacation time was approaching. His girl made it known that
she was going to spend her vacation in Europe. She would go to
Paris first — aboard a French liner.

At first this threw Alec into a panic. He could visualize her
falling for some French Prince Charming. But then the thought
occurred to him — why not go to Paris too? And why not
(secretly, of course) on the same French boat? He would wait until they had put out to sea before he would surprise her by his
presence. (He was fearful she might leave the boat if she knew he
were also going to Paris.)

And so he bought his ticket and waited till the boat was well
under weigh before he announced his presence.

She was indeed surprised, but also delighted. Flattered, no
doubt by such serious attention. And now, wonders to behold,
she really did fall in love with him. It was agreed they would get
married in Paris, soon as they arrived. And they did.

In March, 1930, I arrived in Paris. It was in June of that same

[137]

year that Alec and his Lydia got married in Paris, all unbeknown to me. One day as I am having a drink at the Café du Dôme, who should I see approaching arm in arm but Alec and his girl. Over a couple of Pernods, he recounted all that had happened since I had left for Paris.

We decided to have a marriage feast. I took them to the Coupole just down the street where we had a fabulous repast. They seemed like a very happy couple. I did not see Alec again until about forty years later, when he visited me at my home in Pacific Palisades. He was on his way to Reno to get married again—to the same woman. As she told me later, he was a rather difficult fellow to live with but she could not do without him. To my great surprise, when he was making ready to go he took me aside, held my hand, and embracing me warmly, said, "Hen, you have no idea how happy I am that you made it. I always knew you had it in you."

Set in Baskerville by Charlene McAdams, Santa Barbara;
design and production by Noel Young and Ellen Meske;
printed and bound by R. R. Donnelly & Sons, Crawfordsville, Indiana;
jackets by Rood Associates, Santa Barbara.